Star Wars

SCRAPBOOK

The ESSENTIAL COLLECTION

STEPHEN J. SANSWEET

CHRONICLE BOOKS

SAN FRANCISCO

Printed in Singapore.

Library of Congress Cataloging-in-Publication Data:
Sansweet, Stephen J., 1945–
    Star wars scrapbook : the essential collection /
Stephen J. Sansweet.
            p. cm.
    ISBN 0-8118-2060-2 (hardcover) —
    1. Star Wars films—Collectibles. I. Title.
    PN1995.9.S695S245 1998
    791.43'75—dc21   97-44668
                            CIP

Coordinated by Lucy Autrey Wilson (Lucasfilm)

Edited by Allan Kausch (Lucasfilm)
and Sarah Malarkey (Chronicle Books)

Book design by Earl Gee and Fani Chung,
Gee + Chung Design, San Francisco

Production by Adrian Fernandez
Production assistance by Suzanne Scott

Photography by Kevin Ng

Design direction by Michael Carabetta
(Chronicle Books)

Distributed in Canada by Raincoast Books
8680 Cambie Street
Vancouver, BC V6P 6M9

10 9 8 7 6 5 4 3 2 1

Chronicle Books
85 Second Street
San Francisco, CA 94105

Web Site: www.chronbooks.com

To Josh Ling,

archivist extraordinaire, without whose

help half of these pages would be bare

Collectibles. Ephemera. Just plain stuff.

No matter what you call it, amassing a lot of anything—from barbed wire to Barbie dolls—makes you a collector. Or as my mother used to put it every cleaning day, when she eyed my horde of built-up spaceship model kits, "You're a collector all right, a dust collector!"

Mom looks at my stuff a bit more benignly now, but others invariably ask the questions, **Why collect?** And why *Star Wars*? Much has been written about the psychological underpinnings of collecting, so I needn't retread that ground.

But **why *Star Wars*?** Now that's a question I could answer for days: The wonderful storyline. The incredible visuals. The great one-liners. The battles. The drama. The humor. The ties to primal myths, including those of the hero's search, the wise mentor, the sidekick. The cosmic battle between good and evil. The ultimate redemption of the vilest villain. George Lucas set out to create a new myth for the children of the late 1970s and came up with the ultimate timeless fantasy for us all.

In short, **I love *Star Wars*.** It has literally changed my life, and I'm far from alone. I've seen the original trilogy and the more recent Special Edition countless times. I'm driven by the films, wanting some tangible evidence of their power nearby so that I can be instantly transported back to that galaxy far, far away. It makes hyperspace travel seem a bit slow.

One of the true joys of collecting *Star Wars* stuff is sharing it with others. I've developed close friendships around the world in the last twenty years because of *Star Wars* and because of collecting and showing my collection to others. There's nothing like the look on the face of a first-time visitor. And giving tours of my collection lets me recall interesting stories behind nearly every item.

There isn't time, of course, to take every *Star Wars* fan on a tour. So I've tried to share my passion in other ways, including this book. It's an opportunity to share some of the fun, cool, weird, neat, cosmic, funny, unusual, touching, tasty items that remind us of the first *Star Wars* trilogy, even as George Lucas is hard at work on the much-awaited second trilogy.

A Lucite star. An actor's plaintive appeal on a matchbook cover. A soda-bottle label from Finland. An unusual assortment, yes. But one gathered out of affection for movies that have transcended borders and crossed from the screen into our lives, letting us embrace them in our own way and, to some degree, feel a sense of ownership.

—Steve Sansweet

| 1 9 7 3 | January | George Lucas begins writing what becomes the first of four drafts of the *Star Wars* screenplay. |
| | May | Lucas completes a 13-page plot summary filled with strange names and places, many of which never make it to the final draft. |

| 1 9 7 4 | | Lucas turns down several directing jobs in order to continue developing his space fantasy. |

1 9 7 5	January 28	The second draft of the screenplay is completed. It is titled "The Adventure of the Star Killer."
	June	Lucas hires John Dykstra to do special effects for the film, and Industrial Light & Magic (ILM) is soon formed.
	August 1	The screenplay's third draft is finished.
	November	Three months of casting begin.
	December	Lucas, who has already poured $1 million of his own into the project, gets the official green light from Twentieth Century-Fox.

1 9 7 6	January	Lucas changes the script, killing off Obi-Wan Kenobi.
	January 15	A much-refined fourth draft of the screenplay is completed.
	March 22	Principal photography begins in Tozeur, Tunisia, interrupted four days later by the first winter rainstorm in fifty years.
	July 16	Principal photography wraps, but ILM has completed few useable special effects shots and money is in danger of running out. Fox later provides about half of what Lucas feels he needs to properly complete the film.

1 9 7 7	January	Lucas screens a very rough cut of the film for friends.
	March	John Williams records the *Star Wars* soundtrack music in London.
	April 30	Audiences at the first test screening at the Northpoint Theater in San Francisco respond with enthusiasm.
	May 25	*Star Wars* opens at thirty-two movie theaters in North America, expanding in a few days to more than two hundred theaters. Lines go around the block and *Star Wars* becomes an instant phenomenon.
	August 3	Darth Vader, R2-D2, and C-3PO place their footprints in cement at Mann's Chinese Theater in Hollywood.
	September 16	ABC-TV airs a documentary, *The Making of Star Wars*.
	November	Kenner Products can't produce action figures quickly enough, so it starts selling Early Bird Certificate Packages, a so-called empty box.

1978	February	John Williams wins three Grammy Awards for the *Star Wars* soundtrack. The film receives ten Academy Award nominations.
	March	Veteran writer Leigh Brackett dies of cancer two weeks after completing the first draft of *The Empire Strikes Back* screenplay.
	April	*Star Wars* wins six Academy Awards and gets a seventh Special Achievement Oscar for sound effects creation.
	May	Producer Gary Kurtz scouts northern Europe and selects Finse, Norway, as the location for the Battle of Hoth to open *Empire*.
	May 25	*Star Wars* celebrates its first anniversary with a special poster; the film is still playing in a number of American theaters.
	July	The Official *Star Wars* Fan Club is launched with the first issue of a nameless newsletter, later to be called *Bantha Tracks*.
	July 21	*Star Wars* is rereleased for the first time.
	November 17	The "Star Wars Holiday Special" airs on CBS for the first and—mercifully—last time.
1979	March 5	Principal photography begins at Finse, which is soon cut off from the outside world by a horrendous blizzard, part of the worst winter there in living memory.
	May 22	Filming begins at Elstree Studios for the Rebel Hangar scene on a specially built soundstage that is big enough for a soccer field.
	June 6	Oscar-winning production designer John Barry, just forty-three years old, collapses on the set and dies from a rare form of meningitis.
	August 15	*Star Wars* is rereleased in the United States for the second time.
	August 31	Principal production wraps and a party is held on the Dagobah set.
	September 24	Photography is completed with the shot of the slit tauntaun belly.
	November	John Williams begins composing the score for *Empire*. It is recorded in England in three sessions over the next two months.
1980	May 19	Darth Vader makes the cover of *Time* magazine.
	May 21	*The Empire Strikes Back* is released in North America. It plays to sold out houses in all but 2 of its initial 127 theaters.
	May 28	The novelization of *Empire* sells two million copies in its first week of release.
	June 9	Yoda makes the cover of *People* magazine.
1981	April	*The Empire Strikes Back* wins an Academy Award for Best Sound and a Special Achievement Award for visual effects.
	April 10	*Star Wars* is released in North America for the third time.
	July 31	*Empire* is rereleased in North America.
	September 5	The first of thirteen episodes of the *Star Wars* radio dramatization airs on Public Broadcasting stations in the United States.
	December	The final script for *Revenge of the Jedi* is sent to Elstree Studios, two months behind schedule.

1982	January	Principal photography begins on *Jedi* with a sandstorm scene that is eventually cut.
	February	Harrison Ford suggests that Han Solo die in *Jedi*. George Lucas says thanks, but no thanks.
	April	Location shooting begins in Yuma, Arizona, under the cover name *Blue Harvest*. Local media and some fans uncover the truth, necessitating the hiring of added security.
	April 10	*Star Wars* is released theatrically for the fourth time.
	May 20	Photography wraps on *Jedi* with the filming of part of the speeder bike scene at ILM.
	May	*Star Wars* is released on videocassette for the rental market only. It quickly racks up more than $1 million in rentals, the first video ever to do so.
	November 19	*Empire* is released in theaters for the third time.
1983	January 27	Lucas officially changes the name of his new film to *Return of the Jedi*, although licensees had been told two months before.
	May 25	*Jedi* is released in North American theaters.
1984	January	Lucas gives an R2 unit to the Smithsonian Institution.
	February	*Star Wars* is shown on broadcast television for the first time. Membership in the Official Fan Club peaks at 184,046 members.
	April	*Jedi* wins an Academy Award for Best Visual Effects; it was nominated in four other categories.
1985	March 28	For the first time, the entire trilogy is screened in a triple bill in North America.
	May 25	On the eighth birthday of *Star Wars*, *Jedi* is rereleased.
	September 7	The first season of the *Ewoks and Droids Adventure Hour* animated series begins on ABC TV in the United States.
1986	February 1	*Empire* airs on cable TV in the United States.
	February 25	*Jedi* is released on videocassette.
	September 13	A second season of the animated *Ewoks* starts on ABC.

1 9 8 7	January 9	Star Tours opens at Disneyland; eventually it goes into all four Disney theme parks.
	May 23	The only official *Star Wars* convention, celebrating the film's tenth anniversary, opens at a hotel near the Los Angeles airport. George Lucas attends.
1 9 9 1	May	Author Timothy Zahn's *Heir to the Empire*, the first authorized *Star Wars* novel in years, is published and quickly jumps to number one on the all-important *New York Times* hardcover best-sellers list.
1 9 9 2	March 30	Lucas receives the Irving G. Thalberg Memorial Award from the Academy of Motion Picture Arts and Sciences; his friend Steven Spielberg is the presenter.
1 9 9 4	May	Lucas and Spielberg receive honorary doctorates from the University of Southern California for their contributions to filmmaking.
1 9 9 5	March 4	The *Art of Star Wars* exhibition opens in San Francisco and goes on to break all attendance records.
	April	Plans are firmed up between Lucasfilm and Twentieth Century-Fox for a major video rerelease of technologically upgraded videos, as well as a twentieth anniversary theatrical rerelease of *Star Wars*. Later, *Empire* and *Jedi* are added.
	August 29	The THX remastered *Star Wars* trilogy videocassettes go on sale.
	October	American TV viewers see Darth Vader go up against a new nemesis, the Energizer Bunny, in a clever commercial.
1 9 9 6	January	Work proceeds in earnest to restore the *Star Wars* negative and "fix" scenes that Lucas felt didn't work well the first time.
	January 31	On the last date for retailers to order videos of the original version of the trilogy, the numbers show 22 million cassettes were shipped in North America with another 8 million shipped to other countries.
1 9 9 7	January 19	George Lucas, Mark Hamill, Carrie Fisher, and dozens of costumed characters attend the world premiere of the *Star Wars Special Edition* in West Los Angeles.
	January 31	The *Star Wars Special Edition* opens in North America to a bigger box office in its first weekend than some pundits had been predicting for the entire run of all three special editions.
	June 26	George Lucas shouts "Aaaand action!" as filming begins at England's Leavesden Studios on *Star Wars: Episode I*. Principal photography wraps September 26.
	October 31	*Star Wars: The Magic of Myth* exhibition opens to large crowds at the Smithsonian Institution's National Air and Space Museum. On display are 200 props, costumes, and original art from the trilogy.

Adapted from the Star Wars Insider, *by Jon Bradley Snyder & Allan Kausch. Additional help provided by Darren Reid.*

The original name for George Lucas's epic space fantasy had that extra article, "the," at the beginning. Concept artist Ralph McQuarrie came up with the design—a character that, at the time, merged some of the best of Han Solo and Luke Starkiller, soon to be renamed Skywalker. Some executives at Twentieth Century-Fox weren't crazy about the name ("People might think it's a movie about Clint Eastwood fighting Steve McQueen"), so in a "compromise," one word was dropped. These stickers, and a later version, were used on everything from film cans to file cabinets.

The Revenge of the Jedi *sticker was used on film cans, folders, and other miscellaneous production items as the film was being made. But when George Lucas decided late in 1982 that Jedi don't seek revenge, the stickers became an instant collectible.*

The Star Wars Corporation, P.O. Box 186, San Anselmo, California 94960, Telephone 000—000-0000

Nearly every film is made by an individually named production company for legal and other reasons, and Star Wars was made by The Star Wars Corporation. This is the earliest stationery for the company, whose Northern California headquarters was an old Victorian house in Marin County— basically a place where George Lucas could write his drafts of the script in longhand on blueline pads.

From thousands of light years away come the unusual adventures of Luke Starkiller and his friends as they battle numerous villains and creatures in a galactic civil war. Young Luke is accompanied by his robot companions, R2–D2 and C-3PO; the tough star pilot, Han Solo; and the venerable old warrior Ben Kenobi. The space fantasy involves the search for a kidnapped rebel princess and a confrontation with the dark forces of an evil space empire. George Lucas, director of "American Graffiti," creates a majestic visual experience of extraordinary worlds.

A STAR WARS CORPORATION PRODUCTION

Producer:
GARY KURTZ

Writer/Director:
GEORGE LUCAS

STAR WARS

26
76

TWENTY-SIX FOR SEVENTY-SIX FROM TWENTIETH CENTURY-FOX

After two studios passed, Twentieth Century-Fox agreed to make Star Wars, but it originally thought it would be able to release the film late in 1976. Thus this first solicitation to movie-theater owners in a booklet called "Twenty-Six for Seventy-Six." It uses early black-and-white storyboard-quality art to help describe the "majestic visual experience" of the hero, "Luke Starkiller."

CALENDAR

After the Flaps, McCartney's Wings Airborne

BY ROBERT HILBURN

DENVER—"Rain?" a member of Paul McCartney's stage crew said incredulously as he stared out the back door of the McNichols Arena at the late afternoon downpour. "There's nothing on the schedule today about rain. It must be some mistake."

Another member of the crew even denied, in classic deadpan fashion, that there was any rain. "I don't believe anything until Brian [McCartney's manager, Brian Brolly] tells me. And Brian didn't say anything about rain in Denver."

The sarcasm and humor of the remarks underscored the meticulous planning that has gone into every area of McCartney's first U.S. tour in 10 years. From sound to lighting to media relations, the 21-city tour—which concludes with a three-night stand, beginning Monday, at the Inglewood Forum—has been a carefully designed, faithfully executed campaign. McCartney had simply waited too long for his return to America to leave anything about rain.

With most major rock acts, for instance, the performers might show up for a sound check at the opening tour stop and then again, perhaps, at a few key cities. Generally, however, the band would simply leave it up to the stage crew to make sure everything was ready.

After all, it's a lot more fun holding court back at the hotel or soaking up some sun (a special treat for English bands, which have little chance for a tan back home) than trekking over to the arena to make sure a few monitors are working.

But McCartney, as he had done on each other city on the tour, arrived at the McNichols Arena two hours before show time to test the sound equipment himself, even though the issue of the tour's success was no longer in question.

By the time McCartney had reached Denver—the 16th stop on the tour schedule—he had already accomplished the goal that he had steadfastly pursued, often against discouraging odds, since the day in 1970 that the most successful and influential group in pop music history called it quits.

McCartney, in short, had returned to America—still the financial and prestige cornerstone of the pop music world—and confronted the Beatles legacy without being engulfed by it. His new band, Wings, may not carry either the full musical range and/or sociological impact of the Beatles, but it is a solid, convincing unit. And the concerts, concentrating on post-Beatles material, were rousing, celebrative events. To make it all a bit sweeter, both McCartney's new album ("Wings at the Speed of Sound") and single ("Silly Love Songs") reached No. 1.

The effect of the success, understandably, has been immense on McCartney. But, much like a politician who refuses
Please Turn to Page 76

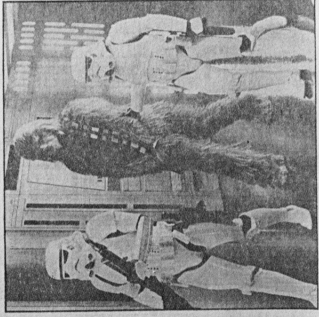

Robots with ape-man captive walk through George Lucas' "Star Wars."

Futurist Film's Tricks to Treat the Eye

BY CHARLES CHAMPLIN

LONDON—The trouble with the future in most futurist movies, George Lucas was saying, is that it always looks new and clean and shiny, as if nobody had ever been there. What is required for true credibility is a used future. The Apollo capsules were instructive in that regard. We were as futuristic as anything we've come up with, but by the time the lads got back from the moon the vehicles were due for a housecleaning and you had the impression that they were littered with shavings, weightless candy wrappers and old Tang jars, hardly more exotic than the family station wagon.

Lucas has built a used future on all eight of the sound stages at EMI's Elstree Studios northwest of London and a further hunk of it on the largest movie stage in all of Western Europe, a few miles away at Shepperton Studios.

He is shooting "Star Wars," a space fantasy he wrote himself. It features Sir Alec Guinness, Harrison Ford, Mark Hamill, and Carrie Fisher (Eddie and Debbie's daughter, lately seen in "Shampoo"). It is about as pure as a fantasy can get, having no points of reference to earth, time or the space with which we are familiar, so that what we watch eventually may not be the future but some galactic past or some alternative, extra-temporal present.

For the convenience of the audience, the characters, as in fairy tales, will speak English, but who knows what queeps and glottals they would get up to, left to their own devices.

In addition to the human look-alikes, both tall and Tin Woodman-seeming and short and keg-shaped, population of robots, there is at least one ape-figure and a whole some speak in British accents.

"I suppose it's science fiction," Lucas says. "But we don't explain anything. We take all the Hardware for granted. The story really is an action adventure, a fantasy, Buck Rogers updated. It's aimed primarily at 14- and 15-year-olds, in the way that 'American Graffiti' was aimed primarily at 16- and 17-year-olds."

It will have lures for the wider audience, as "Graffiti" certainly did, but Lucas is unabashedly making a high-energy, Boy's Own adventure, complete with space pirates, an Imperial Death Star Satellite, good kids and their benevolent protector ranged against the forces of evil, chases, trickeries and hair's breadth 'scapes and a trade in robots who are stolen and sold like terrestrial hubcaps or tape decks.
Please Turn to Page 42

What Getty's Death Means to Museum

BY HENRY J. SELDIS

• The J. Paul Getty Museum in Malibu will become the best-endowed art museum in the country—possibly in the world—once its founder's will passes the usual probate hurdles. But it may take several years before his estate is closed and the museum gets its magnificent inheritance.

According to the will of the 83-year-old oil magnate, who died in England June 6, the museum stands to inherit between $650 and $700 million in Getty Oil Co. stock. By the time the probate is concluded, fluctuations in the stock's market value could considerably alter these figures.

At its present rate, the earnings on that stock would yield $4 million to the museum yearly. But its trustees will have the option to expend capital funds and to reinvest. Prior to his death, Getty had endowed his museum with $40 million. Its budget has been about $2 million annually.

The museum's trustees will meet in the near future to name a new board chairman and a new director, Getty having held both posts. It is expected that deputy director Stephen Garrett will become the museum's director. It is likely that Norris Bramlett, Getty's longtime secretary, will be chosen to become chairman of the museum board on which he has served since its inception.

The Getty Museum also stands to inherit an additional 55 acres of the ranch on which it now occupies 10 acres and the former Getty residence, which served as the initial museum, containing eight galleries, as compared with the present museum which consists of 38 galleries. This would probably make additional parking possible, out of sight of residential neighbors, and also would allow visitors to enter from Pacific Coast Highway and exit toward the back of the ranch, near Sunset Blvd.

Getty started collecting art nearly 50 years ago and from the beginning was interested in three distinct areas: Greek and Roman antiquities, 18th-century French decorative arts and Baroque and Renaissance painting.

The original Getty Museum, housed in his renovated and expanded former residence, opened in 1954, but Getty's acquisitions made expansion necessary by the mid-60s.

In 1974 the new Getty Museum opened in the purported reconstruction of the Villa dei Papiri—a 1st-century Roman villa that was destroyed when Mt. Vesuvius erupted in AD 79. Since the controversial $18-million building opened on its elaborately landscaped grounds, more than 800,000 visitors have come to see its contents—said to be worth $150 million. Admission is free but the museum is
Please Turn to Page 78

Not much advance attention was paid to the hardy—some thought foolish—band of filmmakers preparing Star Wars, which was one of the reasons it took the public by such surprise. But one wise film critic, who knew that the creator of American Graffiti must be up to something interesting, decided to go to England to see for himself. That resulted in this cover story by Charles Champlin in the Sunday Calendar section of the Los Angeles Times, eleven months before Star Wars opened.

Used Future Present and Accounted For

Continued from First Page

It returns Lucas to the genre in which many of us first met him, when he was still a USC graduate student who had made a spectacularly imaginative and assured 20-minute-long future-world drama he called "THX 1138-XEB," in which a Huxleyan man, inadvertently given free will, tries to flee his nightmare world of tomorrow.

That world, which Lucas refers to with amused irony as his $3 billion set, consisted mostly of parking structures and subterranean tunnels in present-day Los Angeles.

"THX-1138" was so impressive that Warners financed a feature-length version of it, which launched Lucas in the commercial world of film-making. It was a cult success and will probably play for a long time, although the addition of a star (Donald Pleasence) and some subplotting did not significantly expand the impact the short film had had.

Although Lucas' talent was obvious, his career after "THX" hung by the thinnest of filaments. He wanted to do a sequel to it but felt that no one ever would. An assist from his close friend Francis Ford Coppola from the days when both were being encouraged by Roger Corman helped him launch "American Graffiti" at Universal. Lucas had to borrow money from friends to complete it and in the time before it was actually released, he was broke and remarkably unwanted. He and his producer-partner Gary Kurtz had been developing "Star Wars" since 1971. Lucas had another picture commitment with Universal, which, however, wanted no part of "Star Wars," nor did United Artists. Fox was not strongly interested either; Lucas says, but by then there had begun to be rumors that "American Graffiti" was something special and, evidently on the strength of them, Fox gambled some development money. "Graffiti" now ranks with the top-grossing movies of all time, and Fox looks to have made a good move.

Inflation over the last three years has doubled the initial budget from $3.5 million to just under $7 million, but, given a hefty shooting schedule plus months of special effects work already under way in Los Angeles, the figure is uncommonly low.

"Seven million dollars," says Gary Kurtz, "but it's like doing a $600,000 epic for Roger Corman." The special effects will take full advantage of some new advances in computer-controlled stop-motion animation. At that, the opticals and miniatures will take $1.5 million of the budget.

"We're trying for a high energy level," Kurtz says, "rather than for the technical perfection of '2001.'" Lucas and his wizard production team—designer John Barry, photographer Gil Taylor, miniaturist John Dykstra, production effects man John Stears, matte artist Peter Ellenshaw—are using every trick not only to generate fantasy but to cut costs, creating a new set from the remnants of the previous set, using partial constructions and forced perspective, and so on.

Even so the hardware is awesome. Half of a star ship, a great semi-circular wedge, its configurations looking battleship gray and rusty, thrusts over half the floor area of one stage. It has been chartered by air heroes for their mission, Kurtz says—apparently from some space rental firm that doesn't try hard enough.

On another stage, a command module takes shape for subsequent shooting. Today the action is at the console of a spherical space station, the Imperial Death Star, which is like a small planet. It is an amazing set, concentric cylinders close to four stories high, linked by several catwalks ideal for a chase sequence (and there is one), the gray bulkheads sliced by illuminated perforations like a computer punch-card on a huge scale.

A white-bearded Alec Guinness, in boots and a shaggy wardrobe and looking more like Uncle Vanya than a senior Buck Rogers, strides to the console, a man in command. The young colleagues are Hamill and Ford, who was in "Graffiti" and also in Coppola's "The Conversation."

The weapons are actually surplus Sterling machine guns, cut down and modified to look spaced-in, but impressively weighty and credible. No plastic ray-guns, thanks. The pieces will kick like mules, credibly, and while there will be nothing like the graphic violence of Sam Peckinpah, there will be action enough to draw a PG rating for what is otherwise a fairy tale. (There are also laser-swords of a splendid futurist lethality.)

Lucas' production notes fondly quote the preface Arthur Conan Doyle wrote for his "The Lost World":

I have wrought my simple plan
If I give one hour of joy
To the boy who's half a man,
Or the man who's half a boy.

That catches Lucas' own enthusiasm for space fantasy. He grew up devouring Buck Rogers and Flash Gordon and is so fond of the form that he runs a gallery-bookstore in New York which specializes in the artifacts of the strips and books that look back at the day after tomorrow. He hopes to open an identical enterprise on the West Coast.

Lucas now lives in San Anselmo as a member of the Marin Movie Mafia—film-makers who no longer see the need to live closer to the exasperations of Hollywood itself. Coppola and his American Zoetrope enterprise was the prime mover, but the informal grouping now also includes Lucas, Michael Ritchie ("Smile," "The Bad News Bears"), Philip Kaufman ("The White Dawn") and John Korty ("Miss Jane Pitman," "Farewell to Manzanar"), who has worked out of San Francisco for years and now has company.

But how many more movies are in Lucas' own future is far from clear.

"The truth is" he says, "that out of what I've made from 'Graffiti' I could, by living fairly modestly, get along without having to earn another dime. And I know that I'm much more a film-maker than a movie director. I do think about retiring to do other things, like the gallery, and special experimental films. I doubt if I'll ever do anything this big again. My personal attitudes are just not prone to this kind of enterprise. I like being a captain rather than a general.

"When the budget goes beyond $2 million or $3 million, another law takes over. You lose the personal touch, the personal contact with every aspect of the movie—unless you're a Kubrick who can take all the time that's required to oversee all the details yourself. You're reliant on others, and they may well be marvelous, but you become more remote than I like to be."

Lucas and Kurtz have in essence rented a vacant studio, on a four-wall deal, and put together their own production team of the brilliant technicians, here and in California, who are, Lucas feels, a vanishing breed. "In 15 or 20 years," Lucas says sadly, "there won't be any big studio pictures of a certain kind, because there won't be anybody who can do the things that have to be done. So much had to be developed for this one, and you had to find people of taste to do it. This time we could still find them. But Peter Ellenshaw, who works mostly for Disney, and Al Whitlock at Universal are the last two giants of the matte artists. Tomorrow—?"

Lucas shrugs.

But for the moment the future is present and accounted for. Not only that, it is so convincing that it is contagious. Ordinary objects take on the guise of tomorrow.

Until now, the "Star Wars" sets have been closed and mystery-shrouded so that you have the sense of walking in a foreign world. You realize with something like chagrin that what could be a magnetic interstellar death cannon is only a carbon-arc lamp, waiting to light a scene.

A very young-looking Mark Hamill, a.k.a. Luke Skywalker, poses before a hand-painted banner (art by Ralph McQuarrie, lettering by Joe Johnston) at Star Wars's "coming out" party at the San Diego Comic Con in the summer of 1976.

S T A R   W A R S
Preview Questionnaire

1 Male _____   Female _____   Profession _____

2 Age: Under 10 _____   11 to 15 _____   16 to 20 _____   21 to 25 _____
         26 to 35 _____   36 to 45 _____   46 to 55 _____   56 & over _____

3 How many times per month do you attend a movie? Less than once _____   One _____
   Two _____   Three _____   Four _____   Five _____   Six _____   Seven _____   More _____

4 What are your all time favorite films? _____

5 Which of the following films have you seen?
   Wizards _____   King Kong _____
   Demon Seed _____   Three Women _____
   Cousin Cousine _____   Welcome to LA _____
   Drive-In _____   Silver Streak _____
   The Late Show _____   Black Sunday _____
   Raggedy Ann and Andy _____   Audrey Rose _____
   Annie Hall _____   American Graffiti _____
   Network _____   Slap Shot _____
   The Valley _____   Airport 77 _____
   THX 1138 _____   Carrie _____
   The Eagle Has Landed _____   Fun With Dick and Jane _____
   In The Realm of the Senses _____   Island in the Stream _____
   Harlan County, U.S.A. _____   The Pink Panther Strikes Again _____
   The Domino Principal _____   Les Zozos _____
   Aloise _____   Rocky _____

6 How would you rate this film? Excellent _____   Good _____   Fair _____   Poor _____

7 Would you recommend it to your friends? _____

8 In what order did you like the characters? (1-6)
   Luke Skywalker _____
   Ben Kenobi _____
   Han Solo _____
   Princess Leia Organa _____
   Governor Moff Tarkin _____
   Darth Vader _____

9 In what order did you like the non-human characters? (1-3)
   Artoo-Detoo (R2-D2) _____
   See Threepio (C-3PO) _____
   Chewbacca the Wookie _____

10 Which other characters did you like? _____

11 Which character did you like best? _____

12 Which scene did you like the best?
   Jawas kidnap Artoo-Detoo and sell the robots. _____
   Luke in the spaceport cantina bar. _____
   Freeing the princess in the Death Star detention area. _____
   Garbage/trashmasher room. _____
   Luke and the princess swing across the metal canyon. _____
   Darth Vader-Ben Kenobi light saber fight. _____
   Escape from the Death Star air battle. _____
   End space battle over Death Star. _____

13 Which other scenes did you like? _____

14 What, if anything, didn't you like about the film? _____

15 Is there any place where the plot was confusing? _____

16 Which "team" did you like best?
   R2-D2 and C-3PO _____
   Han Solo and Chewbacca _____
   Ben Kenobi and Darth Vader _____
   Luke and the Princess _____

17 Had you heard about STAR WARS before the screening?
   Teaser Trailer _____   SF or Comic Fanzines _____   Radio _____
   Comic Book _____   Magazines _____   Television _____
   Novel _____   Newspapers _____   SF or Comic Conventions _____

18 Further comments on back of questionnaire.

Facsimile © 1998 Lucasfilm Ltd.

STAR WARS
Released by 20th Century-Fox

SW-K-55   Luke Skywalker (**MARK HAMILL**) and Han Solo (**HARRISON FORD**) protect Princess Leia (**CARRIE FISHER**) and Chewbacca from an impending Imperial stormtrooper attack.

The Fearsome Foursome: Luke Skywalker, Princess Leia Organa, Chewbacca, and Han Solo strike a pose for photo SW-K-55 for the Star Wars press kit distributed to the print and broadcast media.

This photo of director George Lucas, Chewbacca, and some of the crew looks like it was taken on the set for the final awards ceremony scene in Star Wars. My friend Eric got George to sign it when he visited the set in England for Return of the Jedi.

I SAW STAR WARS™ AT MANN'S CHINESE THEATRE

In case you forgot where you saw Star Wars, or just to brag that you saw it at a grand old-time movie palace in Los Angeles where it opened with 70mm prints two days before its broader release, this bumper sticker is a reminder.

OFFICIAL FIRST DAY COVER

50 YEARS OF TALKING PICTURES

1927 1977

SCIENCE FICTION SERIES

13c USA
50TH ANNIVERSARY YEAR OF TALKING PICTURES

YWOOD. CA
OCT
6
1977
90028

FIRST DAY OF ISSUE

Set N° 2845
of Three Thousand

FIFTY YEARS OF TALKING PICTURES
1927 - 1977
SCIENCE FICTION SERIES

Two of Four

ACADEMY OF SCIENCE FICTION FILMS
Hollywood, California

STAR WARS
(centerpiece)
1977 20th Century-Fox

1936 THE INVISIBLE RAY *Universal*
1939 BUCK ROGERS *Universal*
1940 DR. CYCLOPS *Paramount*

1950 DESTINATION MOON *Eagle-Lion*
1951 THE DAY THE EARTH STOOD STILL *20th Century-Fox*
1951 THE THING *RKO*

Films selected by a committee of the Academy of Science Fiction, Fantasy, and Horror Films, Dr. Donald A. Reed, President. Enclosure
commentary by Douglas Menville. Photos courtesy of Collectors Book Store, 6763 Hollywood Boulevard, Hollywood, California 90028.
design/j. mass-dycom

The first day of issue for a stamp commemorating fifty years of talking pictures was celebrated by the nonprofit Academy of Science Fiction Films with this first-day cover featuring Luke Skywalker surrounded by some classic sci-fi and fantasy film images.

HOW TO ATTACH YOUR MASK

Separate mask from surround.
Push out eyeholes.
Fold as indicated and attach
elastic bands
(or string) and
loop over ears.

Lyons Maid

STAR WARS™

Lyons Maid, which has made delicious ice cream in England for years, hooked up with Star Wars to offer four paper punch-out masks. In addition to C-3PO here, the masks included Chewbacca, Darth Vader, and a stormtrooper. Finding a complete unpunched set these days is very difficult.

Kenner's famous—or infamous—"empty box" came in for some media criticism at Christmas 1977, but it turned out to be a bargain. Unable to ship any action figures the year that Star Wars came out because of the long lead times needed, Kenner sold this Early Bird Certificate Package.

NO. 38140

PRICE

STAR WARS

EARLY BIRD CERTIFICATE PACKAGE

For a limited time only — not to be sold after December 31, 1977

INCLUDES:

★ EARLY BIRD CERTIFICATE — good for 4 authentically detailed STAR WARS Action Figures

★ Colorful Display Stand with STAR WARS Picture

★ STAR WARS Club Membership Card

★ STAR WARS Stickers

WHAT YOU DO:

MAIL IN . . .
the postage paid Early Bird Certificate

RECEIVE . . .
between FEBRUARY 1 - JUNE 1, 1978, before they're available in stores, posable Action Figures of: Luke Skywalker," Princess Leia," Chewbacca," and Artoo-Detoo"(see back of package for full details).

AGES 4 AND UP

Kenner

PROOF-OF-PURCHASE COUPON
TEAR OFF AND SAVE THIS COUPON

Your STAR WARS Action Figures will be mailed, post-paid, between February 1, 1978 and June 1, 1978. If you have not received them by June 1, 1978, please mail your inquiry to the address shown on the reverse side of this coupon.

DATE MAILED *December 12, 1977*

MAY THE FORCE BE WITH YOU.™

STAR WARS™

323-028-00

©1977 TWENTIETH CENTURY FOX FILM CORP.

It included a mail-in coupon for the first four action figures, some stickers, a membership card for a nonexistent Star Wars Space Club (signed by Luke himself!), and a cardboard display stand for the first twelve action figures.

The stars of STAR WARS™

Authentic looking action figures from the smash hit movie

Start your own collection with an Early Bird Set

With this Special Certificate Package, you can be sure of owning a set of the first authentic STAR WARS figures available.

Inside, there's an Early Bird Certificate that you mail in to get one of the first sets made. Your set will be mailed to you, postage paid, as soon as it's ready... between February 1, and June 1, 1978.

The Early Bird Set includes these 4 sturdy plastic, posable figures:

Luke Skywalker™ (3¾ inches high) with a Light Saber™ which slides out of its hand held case ready for action with the flick of a special lever in Luke's arm.

Princess Leia Organa™ (3½ inches high with her special Star Puffs™ hairdo, a removable cape and a Laser pistol™ like the one she used in the movie.

R2-D2 (Artoo-Detoo)™ (2¼ inches high) with movable legs and a head that "clicks" as it turns around.

Chewbacca™ (4¼ inches high) with his special Laser Rifle™ and ammunition belt across his chest.

Later, once they're available in stores, you'll be able to add the other 8 stars of STAR WARS to your collection, and use them all with Kenner's galaxy of other STAR WARS toys and spaceships.

HOW TO ORDER:

1. Fill in your name and address on both areas of the Certificate card.

2. Tear off the proof-of-purchase coupon from the Early Bird Certificate and keep it. It's your record that you've mailed in your Early Bird Certificate.

3. Mail the Certificate, *no postage necessary*. Be sure to note the date you mailed your Certificate.

4. Next, set up the display stand that comes with this package (see Instructions for Assembly below).

5. *Between February 1 and June 1, 1978,* you will receive your set of 4 figures. Included with the figures is a complete set of holders for your entire collection. The holders keep the figures on the stand for display . . . yet, allow them to be easily removed for hours of STAR WARS play.

Contents: Early Bird Certificate, Display Stand, STAR WARS Membership Card, Stickers and Photos.

1. Detach photos, membership card, and information card at perforations.

2. Carefully bend the back of stage up at the score line. Slide backstage tabs into the slots on stage floor.
When your STAR WARS figures arrive, the package will contain your four figures and a complete set of plastic holders to display your entire collection of STAR WARS figures.

CHARACTERS: ©1977 TWENTIETH CENTURY FOX FILM CORP. GENERAL MILLS FUN GROUP, INC. 1977 by its Division, KENNER PRODUCTS, Cincinnati, Ohio 45202   figures made in Hong Kong   "STAR WARS" AND CHARACTER NAMES ARE TRADEMARKS OF TWENTIETH CENTURY FOX FILM CORP. KENNER PRODUCTS, CINCINNATI, OHIO 45202

The Fan Club has always been a great place to get Star Wars merchandise, some of it exclusive. Here is the first membership card and first cloth patch. The two small pinback metal badges are from a larger set of fourteen, but are unusual because one features the Fan Club logo and the other the face of writer/director George Lucas. The larger badge, picturing a Tatooine bantha, was given to Fan Club members who brought in new members, making them "Rebel recruiters."

CHARTER MEMBER

OFFICIAL STAR WARS FAN CLUB

MAY THE FORCE BE WITH YOU

Name _____

Force # _____

FACTORS ETC., INC., BEAR, DEL. U.S.A. IMAGE FACTORY INC., HOLLYWOOD, CALIF.   PRINTED IN U.S.A.   © 1977 TWENTIETH CENTURY FOX

The first issue of the Official Star Wars Fan Club newsletter came out in 1978. There wasn't much notice initially, so the first four Fan Club newsletters (later compiled into one large issue) are extremely hard to find. This one has a biography of George Lucas and word about when filming would start on "Star Wars II," as well as some of the filmmaking secrets behind Star Wars.

THE STAR WARS

The Strange Item in your Membership Kit

Some members of the club have written in and asked about the triangular decal included in the Membership Kit. They want to know the significance of the figure, and what he has to do with *Star Wars*.

We included this particular decal, painted by Production Illustrator Ralph McQuarrie, to lend a sense of history to the club. It's been around just about the longest, and has always been used to represent *Star Wars*.

We called up Ralph McQuarrie and asked him about the decal. "It was done as a symbol for the film—to go on film cans and letters. George had had one for *American Graffiti*, and wanted one for *Star Wars*." It's been used to identify things as being a part of *Star Wars*. It can be found on notebooks, file cabinets, and doors. A simplified version of McQuarrie's design can be seen on the stationery used by Star Wars Corporation.

"It was done while we were working on costumes," said McQuarrie. "This was how we first pictured Han Solo. It could be a sort of Luke character, but I think it's more like Han. Anyway, later George decided that Han Solo should be a more relaxed character, and his costume was changed. But this decal was designed before the change."

Perhaps more than any other piece of artwork, this design has come to mean *Star Wars*.

The Newsletter of the Official *Star Wars* Fan Club, volume one, number 1. Published bi-monthly, in February, April, June, August, October, and December, by Factors Etc. Inc. of Bear, Delaware. Entire contents copyright 1978 Twentieth Century-Fox Film Corporation. Edited by Craig Miller. Copies available to members of the Official Star Wars Fan Club.

STAR WARS FAN CLUB
P.O. Box 1000, Beverly Hills, Ca. 90213

Facsimile © 1998 Lucasfilm Ltd.

STAR WARS

How did you come up with the 'droids, and were they robots or real people?

The two 'droids, R2-D2 and C-3PO, are among George Lucas's favorite characters. In fact, an earlier version of the script had the two robots as the main characters, instead of the humans.

The robots were built from designs prepared by Ralph McQuarrie, Production Illustrator for Star Wars, following detailed discussions with George Lucas.

John Stears, Special Production and Mechanical Effects Supervisor, is the one who made most of the robots work. He and his staff talked with various experts in robotics, the science of robots, prior to building the first one. Besides the dozen robots he built, he also came up with the light sabers and land vehicles.

C-3PO was the only robot not built by Stears. He was designed by Ralph McQuarrie, Art Director Norman Reynolds, and Sculptress Liz Moore. C-3PO's casing was sculpted to fit actor Anthony Daniels, who played C-3PO throughout the movie.

Several different versions of R2-D2 appeared in the film. One version had actor Kenny Baker inside. Other versions were built for special functions, including several operated by remote control.

Where did George Lucas get the idea for Star Wars, and why did he do it?

George Lucas had long been a fan of science fiction and action-adventure books and films. As early as 1971, he wanted to make a space fantasy film. Originally, he wanted to make a Flash Gordon movie but was unable to obtain the rights to the character. Instead, he researched where Alex Raymond, who had done the Flash Gordon comic strips, had gotten his inspiration. Discovering that Raymond was influenced by the books of Edgar Rice Burroughs, Mr. Lucas read through Burroughs's John Carter of Mars series of books. Further research led to the fact that Burroughs was inspired by a science fantasy called Gulliver on Mars, written by Edwin Arnold and published in 1905.

George Lucas made Star Wars because "I really enjoy the space fantasy genre. It's a lot of fun. I really wanted to make Star Wars in the hope that it will be such a fantastic success everyone will want to copy it. Then I'll get to see space fantasy movies and won't have to do them. I'll finally be able to sit back and enjoy other people's space adventures."

For more information on George Lucas and his background, read the article on him elsewhere in this issue.

How did you get the Light Sabers to work?

The problem of getting the Light Sabers to work fell upon Special Production and Mechanical Effects Supervisor John Stears. Production Illustrator Ralph McQuarrie gave Stears a sketch of what the Light Sabers should look

like when in use, and, based on that, he made them work.

The 'handles' of the Light Sabers are seven inches long, and one inch in diameter. Loosely attached to a person's belt for carrying, when pulled from the belt and activated, there is a four foot long burst of light and an accompanying hum of power.

The 'blade' part of the Light Saber is actually a four-sided blade attached to a small motor in the handle. The motor is used to quickly rotate the blade.

Two sides of the blade are coated with a highly reflective material similar to the material used on motion picture screens. One of those two sides is painted four inches higher than the other side. When spinning, this gave the blade its flashing effect.

A device was made to lock a light source onto the camera, allowing the camera both to move freely and to be aligned with the light source and the blade's reflection.

The film was then taken to a special effects house and rotoscoped, an animation process involving the frame-by-frame drawing of previously photographed live action. This animation process added brightness, flash, and color to the Light Saber blades.

That's all for this issue. Next issue, we'll answer more questions about the how and why of Star Wars.

Star Wars Merchandise and Discounts

As you all are probably aware, there is a lot of Star Wars-related merchandise on the market—tee-shirts, posters, blankets, masks, towels, toys, and more. And we've received quite a few letters from people wanting to know what is being produced and where it's available.

Some future issues of the newsletter will have inserts from companies producing Star Wars merchandise. Not only will these inserts serve to let you know what items are available and where they can be ordered, but some of the companies will provide discounts to members of the Official Star Wars Fan Club.

So look to future issues of this newsletter for information and discounts on Star Wars products.

STAR WARS

Local Chapters for the Official *Star Wars* Fan Club

We've received dozens of letters from people who'd like to start their own *Star Wars* Fan Club. They want to get together with people who share their interests. And we've decided to help them.

We'll be running listings of all of the Local Chapters, to let you know if there's one in your area. We'll also run write-ups on Local Chapter activities.

We've set up some guidelines for the formation and running of Local Chapters. If you're interested in forming one, write to Local Chapters; c/o *Star Wars* Fan Club; P.O. Box 1000; Beverly Hills, CA 90213.

Star Wars II

Almost since the day *Star Wars* was released, rumours about the making and release of *Star Wars II* have been spreading. The ones we've heard announce the film as being in at least five different stages of production, give four different 'firm' dates for the opening of the film, and other information that bears little or no resemblance to reality.

To keep you informed of what's actually happening, we'll be running a semi-regular feature on *Star Wars II*. We'll let you know about production and release dates, casting, scripting, and everything else concerned with the making of the sequel.

As things stand right now, production on *Star Wars II* should start in early 1979, with the release tentatively scheduled for the first quarter of 1980. Many of the characters—Luke Skywalker, Princess Leia Organa, and Han Solo—will be returning, along with R2-D2, C-3PO, Darth Vader, and probably Chewbacca.

Star Wars Cast & Crew Find Mutual Interest: Comic Books

"Sometimes I really felt illiterate around the set," said Mark Hammil, *Star Wars*' Luke Skywalker. However, it wasn't discussing Shakespeare with Alec Guinness that made him feel unread, it was discussing comic books with aficionado George Lucas.

Mark explained his love for comic books. "When I was a kid, we weren't allowed to have them in my family. I was told they were a waste of money. But I still got them somehow. That made them even more exciting to read because they were forbidden. And my friends all had them. My love for them now is a kind of compensation for not being able to buy them then. I have collected a lot of them now, like *Silver Surfer*. I love Green Lantern—the one with the ring. Superman got on my nerves, but I like Batman because he could get killed. And I got my fix of monsters from *Classics Illustrated*, which had things like Frankenstein."

George Lucas was so passionate about comics as a boy that Alex Raymond's *Flash Gordon* was the inspiration for *Star Wars*. His love of the genre has remained so constant that he co-owns a gallery-bookstore in New York City which specializes in space fantasy and science fiction comic strips and comic books.

Carrie Fisher is also a devotee of comic books, but her taste runs more to "those love comics. I still have them, and I am still fascinated by them. They gave dating tips, which was my favorite section. There was *True Love, Young Romance*, and *Just Married*. They had the most delightfully bizarre stories. I read them twice as soon as I got them. They were always the same and always great. Love, conflict, and then back together again. Romeo and Juliet stuff, but it always worked.

"There's also another series that I loved," said Carrie. "It was underground comic types of things, like *Slime and Despair*. I didn't really read them. I just loved to look at their covers. I think my favorite was the *Leather Nun*. And you had to be eighteen to buy it."

Even producer Gary Kurtz was not immune to the comic book mania on the *Star Wars* set. "Sometimes Gary would get an excited little grin," Mark Hamill recalled, "and he'd start talking about Scrooge McDuck and the other Carl Barks creations."

Q & A

In each issue of the newsletter, we'll try to answer some of the most-often-asked questions about *Star Wars*. If you have any questions that you'd like to have answered, send them to Q & A; c/o *Star Wars* Fan Club; P.O. Box 1000; Beverly Hills, CA 90213. We don't have room to answer all of the questions we receive, but we'll answer as many as we can in these pages.

P.O. Box 1000, Beverly Hills, Ca. 90213

GEORGE LUCAS: The Man Behind *Star Wars*

George Lucas is among the new generation of young film directors who have loved films all their life. These young directors were brought up on motion pictures, and continued their romance with film by attending film schools. They studied theories of filmmaking, explored the technical demands by making their own short films, and endlessly viewed old films to rediscover the visual and narrative elements that made moviegoing a weekly habit.

Other members of this new generation include Francis Ford Coppola (*The Godfather*, and *The Godfather, Part II*), Steven Spielberg (*Jaws*, and *Close Encounters of the Third Kind*), Brian De Palma (*Phantom of the Paradise*, and *Carrie*), John Milius (*The Wind and The Lion*, and *Dillinger*), and Martin Scorcese (*Taxi Driver*, and *New York, New York*). All of these men share the love for films that made George Lucas want to become a director.

George Lucas was born on May 14, 1944. The son of a retail merchant, he was raised on a walnut ranch in Modesto, California. As a teenager, his two passions were art and cars. Determined to become a champion race car driver, he worked at rebuilding cars at a foreign car garage and in pit crews at races throughout the country. Following a serious automobile accident a few weeks prior to his high school graduation, he gave up all hope of becoming a race car driver.

He attended Modesto Junior College for two years, where he majored in social sciences. By chance, he met award-winning cinematographer Haskell Wexler, who encouraged him to study filmmaking, and helped pave the way for his admittance to the University of Southern California Film School.

While attending the USC Film School, he quickly turned out eight short films. He subsequently became a teaching assistant for a class training U.S.

Navy cameramen. With half of the class assisting him, he made a science fiction short entitled *Electronic Labyrinth (THX 1138:4EB)*. The film won the Third National Student Film Festival in 1967–68, and several other awards.

In 1967, he was one of four students selected to make short films about the making of Carl Foreman's *McKenna's Gold*. His short was Foreman's favorite, although it told more about the mysteries of the desert than about Foreman's film. Lucas then won a scholarship to Warner Bros. to observe the making of *Finian's Rainbow*, under the direction of Francis Ford Coppola.

While working as Coppola's assistant on *The Rain People*, he made a forty minute documentary about the making of the movie, entitled *Filmmaker*, which has been recognized as one of the best films on filmmaking.

George Lucas's first professional feature motion picture, *THX 1138*, was an expanded version of his prize-winning student film. Starring Robert Duvall and Donald Pleasence, it was enthusiastically received by critics when it was first released, and has since become a cult film with a large following.

In 1973, he co-wrote (with Gloria Katz and Willard Huyck) and directed *American Graffiti*. Upon its release, *American Graffiti* was hailed as the quintessential movie about American teenage life and rituals. The movie was nominated for five Academy Awards and won the Golden Globe Award for Best Motion Picture—Comedy, and both the New York Film Critics and the National Society of Film Critics Awards for Best Screenplay.

George met his wife, Marcia, when she was hired to assist him on editing a documentary under the supervision of Verna Fields. Marcia Lucas was one of the editors on *Star Wars*, and was nominated for the Academy Award for Best Editing, with Verna Fields, for *American Graffiti*. She has also edited *Alice Doesn't Live Here Anymore* and *Taxi Driver*.

Kenner's 3¾-inch Star Wars action figures are at the heart of most Star Wars collections. The toy company promoted them—and the rest of its line—with small booklets inserted into vehicles and other toys. Here's a spread promoting the first twelve figures, noting that their heights range from 2¼ inches (Jawa) to 4¼ inches (Chewbacca).

The Burger Chef fast-food hamburger chain, in conjunction with the Coca-Cola Co., had one of the first Star Wars promotional tie-ins. There were seven different Funmeal boxes that could be turned into everything from C-3PO and R2-D2 punch-out puppets to X-wings and TIE fighters, a landspeeder, and two games.

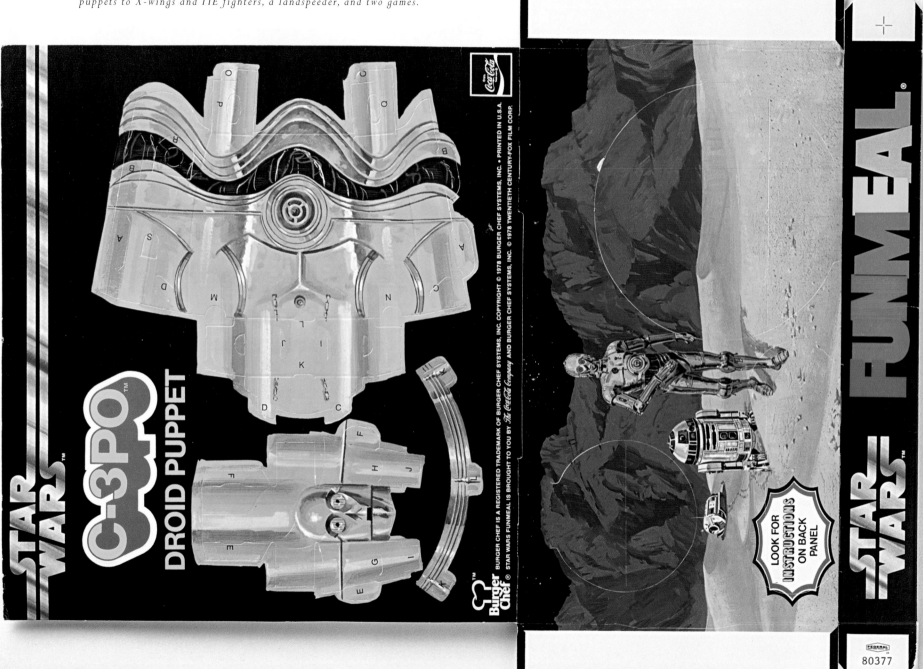

FUNMEAL®

C-3PO™ ASSEMBLY INSTRUCTIONS

1. REMOVE ALL PARTS FROM CARTON.

2. FOLD BODY AT SCORES AND LOCK TABS A-B-C-D-O
   INTO SLOTS A-B-C-D-O.

3. FOLD HEAD AT SCORES AND LOCK TABS E-F
   INTO SLOT E-F.

4. INSERT HEAD ON BODY — TABS I-J INTO SLOTS I-J.

5. PLACE COLLAR AROUND NECK — INSERT TABS L-K-K
   INTO L-K-K.

6. INSERT HEAD STRAP G-H INTO SLOTS G-H ON
   SIDES OF HEAD.

7. FOLD ARMS AT SCORES — FOLD TABS M-N AND
   INSERT INTO SLOTS M-N ON BODY.

8. FOLD LEGS AT SCORES — FOLD TABS P-Q AND INSERT
   INTO HOLES P-Q AT BOTTOM OF BODY.

9. PULL OUT TAB R — REMOVE CENTER — PUSH
   DRINKING STRAW THROUGH HOLE AND UP TO TABS S
   — INSERT TAB S IN OPEN END OF STRAW.

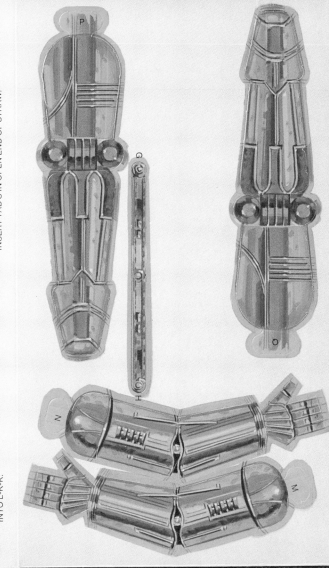

FUNMEAL®

Darth Vader and his loyal stormtroopers weren't above doing promotion for Star Wars, helping to ensure its world-wide fame. Here, the Dark Lord of the Sith and his aides seem to be awaiting a double-decker London bus to take them to Harrods for shopping. The passengers seem a bit leery.

BEST WISHES

Anthony Daniels
C3PO

Kellogg's
C-3PO's

NEW!
CRUNCHY
HONEY-FLAVOURED
OAT, WHEAT & CORN
CEREAL

NOUVEAU!
CÉRÉALES
CROUSTILLANTES D'AVOINE
DE BLÉ ET DE MAÏS
AROMATISÉES DE MIEL

3PO IS HUMAN !

Greetings from

British actor Anthony Daniels was perfect for the part of C-3PO, the fussy golden droid who was one of the key characters in the trilogy and subsequent merchandising, capped with his own cereal (here in a snack-pack box from Canada). But he did the role so well that the crew making the film often forgot that there was a man inside the suit and behind the mask. So Tony printed up a reminder on matchbook covers that he placed on cast and crew buffet tables. "They thanked me for the matches, but most of them didn't get my point," he says.

The Japanese have a sweet tooth and love
small presents with their candy, such as those
found in Cracker Jacks boxes in the U.S. The competitors Morinaga and Meiji produced a
wide variety of attractive Star Wars packages and some great mini-premiums.

*There were dimensional characters and polyester vehicles, which needed
some assembly but moved well on tiny wheels; plastic bookmarks and
pinback badges, some with lenticular lenses that changed the image; and
plastic photo or art tags, rub-down transfers, and tiny boxes with Star Wars characters or vehicles.*

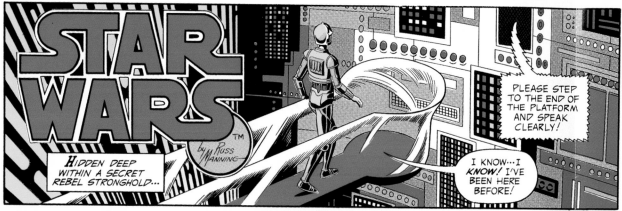

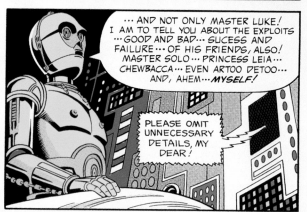

The *Star Wars comic strip started appearing in daily and Sunday papers in March 1979, helping to bridge the gap until the next film was ready. Black Falcon Ltd., the Lucasfilm entity that was making The Empire Strikes Back along with Chapter II Company, sent a notice and copy of the first Sunday episode to licensees. Dark Horse Comics has reprinted much of this classic early work.*

The Los Angeles Times began syndication of the "Star Wars" comic

strip in March, 1979, to approximately 214 newspapers. The comic

strip, written and drawn by Russ Manning, was developed by Black

Falcon over a period of one year. We are sure you will agree

that bringing the characters to the public everyday is a terrific

reminder that "Star Wars" is an ongoing property.

For your reference, the following lists the papers carrying the

daily and Sunday strip in the United States and Canada.

A LUCASFILM, LTD. COMPANY

P.O. BOX 8669, UNIVERSAL CITY, CALIFORNIA 91608   TELEPHONE (000) 000-0000

Los Angeles Times SYNDICATE

STAR WARS™

By Archie Goodwin and Al Williamson

RELEASE SEPTEMBER 6, 7, 8 1982

By Archie Goodwin and Al Williamson

By Archie Goodwin and Al Williamson

By Archie Goodwin and Al Williamson

VISAS

CORELLIA

UTAPAU

A.C. No. B948-OH 117

VISAS

104A-102

INTERGALACTIC PASSPORT

0230

Security was tight on the British set of The Empire Strikes Back, *but there were VIP guests and others who came for visits. So producer Gary Kurtz had hard-cased Intergalactic Passports made up as both a welcome and a souvenir. They were so popular that they later became the basis for a commercial* Star Wars *passport sold at bookstores.*

Lucasfilm's Los Angeles office had been in a small bungalow on the Universal Studios lot. But with the success of Star Wars, it quickly outgrew the space, and in September 1979 it moved down the street in North Hollywood to a beautifully renovated old brick building called the Egg Company. Illustrator Ralph McQuarrie came up with the perfect illustration to mark the move.

WE'RE MOVING!

Our Los Angeles office renovation is completed
and as of September 1979 we will be located at:

3855 Lankershim Boulevard
North Hollywood, California 91604

Telex: #194505 LUCASFILM UVSL

THE LUCASFILM FAMILY

Chapter II Company

Black Falcon Ltd.

Radio Pictures, Inc.

The Star Wars Corporation

Industrial Light & Magic, Inc.

Sprocket Systems, Inc.

Lucasfilm Ltd.

With offices in San Francisco, Los Angeles, London

Medway Productions, Inc.

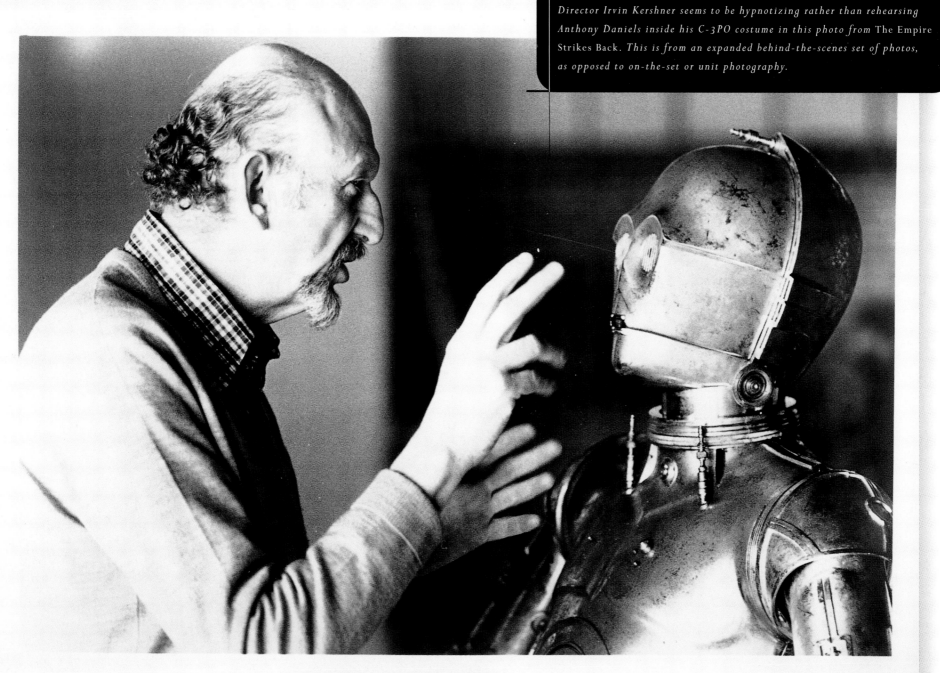

Director Irvin Kershner seems to be hypnotizing rather than rehearsing Anthony Daniels inside his C-3PO costume in this photo from The Empire Strikes Back. This is from an expanded behind-the-scenes set of photos, as opposed to on-the-set or unit photography.

"THE EMPIRE STRIKES BACK"
Released by 20th Century-Fox

ESB 102   Director Irvin Kershner rehearses C-3PO **(ANTHONY DANIELS)** for a scene in "The Empire Strikes Back."

Nobody did very much for the opening of the unheralded Star Wars. But by the time The Empire Strikes Back premiered, there were galas galore. This unusual-looking Darth Vader was the cover for an invitation to a benefit screening ($100 a head) for the Crossroads School in West Los Angeles, where the producer's children just happened to go. Guests at the buffet supper that followed found a party favor at their seats: a sparkling, carved Lucite star in a blue velvet bag.

The Empire Strikes Back *as seen through a spaceship porthole? Not quite. It's a set of six cardboard discs from Canada's York Peanut Butter jars. Trading cards come in many sizes, but round ones are fairly uncommon.*

The cardbacks, in both English and French, featured an offer for a Darth Vader "Action Poster" for only $2 and a proof of purchase. Sorry, but the offer expired January 1, 1981.

5. See-Threepio (C-3PO) expresses his concern to Princess Leia that Master Luke is missing in the freezing cold night on Hoth.

STAR WARS™ POSTER OFFER
"Special Star Wars **Darth Vader** Action Poster" size 16"X 20", full colour. To order send a cheque or money order for $2.00 payable to: Star Wars Poster Offer together with 1 proof of purchase (liner or label) from York, Smoothy or Crunchy Peanut Butter to: Star Wars Poster Offer, Box 41, Station 'G', Toronto, Ontario M4M 3E8. Offer expires January 1, 1981.

5. See-Threepio (C-3PO) fait part à la princesse Leia de son inquiétude au sujet de Luke, disparu dans la nuit glaciale de Hoth.

OFFRE D'AFFICHE 'STAR WARS'™
Affiche spéciale en couleurs 'Star Wars' représentant **Darth Vader** en action. Dimension: 16X20 pouces. Pour commander l'affiche, veuillez envoyer un chèque ou mandat-poste de $2.00 payable à: Offre d'affiche 'Star Wars' accompagné d'une preuve d'achat (parchemin ou étiquette) d'un bocal de beurre d'arachides York, Smoothy ou Crunchy, à: Offre d'affiche 'Star Wars', Case postale 41, Succursale 'G', Toronto, Ontario, M4M 3E8. L'offre prend fin le 1er janvier 1981.

TM: ©LFL 1980/Canada Packers Inc., authorized user.
TM: ©LFL 1980/Usager autorisé: Canada Packers Inc.

Facsimile © 1998 Lucasfilm Ltd.

---

4. Chewbacca, the Wookiee co-pilot of the Millennium Falcon, braces himself against the cold wind on the icy plains of the planet Hoth.

STAR WARS™ POSTER OFFER
"Special Star Wars **Darth Vader** Action Poster" size 16"X 20", full colour. To order send a cheque or money order for $2.00 payable to: Star Wars Poster Offer together with 1 proof of purchase (liner or label) from York, Smoothy or Crunchy Peanut Butter to: Star Wars Poster Offer, Box 41, Station 'G', Toronto, Ontario M4M 3E8. Offer expires January 1, 1981.

4. Chewbacca, le co-pilote Wookiee du Millennium Falcon, s'arme de tout son courage pour affronter le vent froid des plaines gelées de la planète Hoth.

OFFRE D'AFFICHE 'STAR WARS'™
Affiche spéciale en couleurs 'Star Wars' représentant **Darth Vader** en action. Dimension: 16X20 pouces. Pour commander l'affiche, veuillez envoyer un chèque ou mandat-poste de $2.00 payable à: Offre d'affiche 'Star Wars' accompagné d'une preuve d'achat (parchemin ou étiquette) d'un bocal de beurre d'arachides York, Smoothy ou Crunchy, à: Offre d'affiche 'Star Wars', Case postale 41, Succursale 'G', Toronto, Ontario, M4M 3E8. L'offre prend fin le 1er janvier 1981.

TM: ©LFL 1980/Canada Packers Inc., authorized user.
TM: ©LFL 1980/Usager autorisé: Canada Packers Inc.

Facsimile © 1998 Lucasfilm Ltd.

---

1. Darth Vader entreats Luke Skywalker to embrace the dark side of the Force and give in to his anger and hatred. "Join me, and together we will rule the Galaxy", promises the evil agent of the Empire.

STAR WARS™ POSTER OFFER
"Special Star Wars **Darth Vader** Action Poster" size 16"X 20", full colour. To order send a cheque or money order for $2.00 payable to: Star Wars Poster Offer together with 1 proof of purchase (liner or label) from York, Smoothy or Crunchy Peanut Butter to: Star Wars Poster Offer, Box 41, Station 'G', Toronto, Ontario M4M 3E8. Offer expires January 1, 1981.

1. Darth Vader supplie Luke Skywalker de se ranger de son côté de la Force et de céder à sa colère et sa haine. "Joins-toi à moi et ensemble nous gouvernerons la Galaxie", promet le malfaisant agent de l'Empire.

OFFRE D'AFFICHE 'STAR WARS'™
Affiche spéciale en couleurs 'Star Wars' représentant **Darth Vader** en action. Dimension: 16X20 pouces. Pour commander l'affiche, veuillez envoyer un chèque ou mandat-poste de $2.00 payable à: Offre d'affiche 'Star Wars' accompagné d'une preuve d'achat (parchemin ou étiquette) d'un bocal de beurre d'arachides York, Smoothy ou Crunchy, à: Offre d'affiche 'Star Wars', Case postale 41, Succursale 'G', Toronto, Ontario, M4M 3E8. L'offre prend fin le 1er janvier 1981.

TM: ©LFL 1980/Canada Packers Inc., authorized user.
TM: ©LFL 1980/Usager autorisé: Canada Packers Inc.

Facsimile © 1998 Lucasfilm Ltd.

---

3. With only the lights of his crashed X-wing to show the way, the lost and frightened Luke Skywalker peers through the Dagobah fog in search of Yoda, the Jedi Master.

STAR WARS™ POSTER OFFER
"Special Star Wars **Darth Vader** Action Poster" size 16"X 20", full colour. To order send a cheque or money order for $2.00 payable to: Star Wars Poster Offer together with 1 proof of purchase (liner or label) from York, Smoothy or Crunchy Peanut Butter to: Star Wars Poster Offer, Box 41, Station 'G', Toronto, Ontario M4M 3E8. Offer expires January 1, 1981.

3. Aidé uniquement par les lumières de son aéronef à aile X fracassé pour trouver sa route, Luke Skywalker, perdu et effrayé, sonde le brouillard Dagobah à la recherche de Yoda, le maître Jedi.

OFFRE D'AFFICHE 'STAR WARS'™
Affiche spéciale en couleurs 'Star Wars' représentant **Darth Vader** en action. Dimension: 16X20 pouces. Pour commander l'affiche, veuillez envoyer un chèque ou mandat-poste de $2.00 payable à: Offre d'affiche 'Star Wars' accompagné d'une preuve d'achat (parchemin ou étiquette) d'un bocal de beurre d'arachides York, Smoothy ou Crunchy à: Offre d'affiche 'Star Wars', Case postale 41, Succursale 'G', Toronto, Ontario, M4M 3E8. L'offre prend fin le 1er janvier 1981.

TM: ©LFL 1980/Canada Packers Inc., authorized user.
TM: ©LFL 1980/Usager autorisé: Canada Packers Inc.

Facsimile © 1998 Lucasfilm Ltd.

---

6. Too-Onebee (2-1B), the surgeon droid, in the Rebel base medical centre on the planet Hoth.

STAR WARS™ POSTER OFFER
"Special Star Wars **Darth Vader** Action Poster" size 16"X 20", full colour. To order send a cheque or money order for $2.00 payable to: Star Wars Poster Offer together with 1 proof of purchase (liner or label) from York, Smoothy or Crunchy Peanut Butter to: Star Wars Poster Offer, Box 41, Station 'G', Toronto, Ontario M4M 3E8. Offer expires January 1, 1981.

6. Too-Onebee (2-1B), le chirurgien, au centre médical de la base des rebelles de la planète Hoth.

OFFRE D'AFFICHE 'STAR WARS'™
Affiche spéciale en couleurs 'Star Wars' représentant **Darth Vader** en action. Dimension: 16X20 pouces. Pour commander l'affiche, veuillez envoyer un chèque ou mandat-poste de $2.00 payable à: Offre d'affiche 'Star Wars' accompagné d'une preuve d'achat (parchemin ou étiquette) d'un bocal de beurre d'arachides York, Smoothy ou Crunchy à: Offre d'affiche 'Star Wars', Case postale 41, Succursale 'G', Toronto, Ontario, M4M 3E8. L'offre prend fin le 1er janvier 1981.

TM: ©LFL 1980/Canada Packers Inc., authorized user.
TM: ©LFL 1980/Usager autorisé: Canada Packers Inc.

Facsimile © 1998 Lucasfilm Ltd.

---

2. C-3PO and R2-D2 anxiously await news of the missing Luke Skywalker, lost on the frigid wastelands of Hoth.

STAR WARS™ POSTER OFFER
"Special Star Wars **Darth Vader** Action Poster" size 16"X 20", full colour. To order send a cheque or money order for $2.00 payable to: Star Wars Poster Offer together with 1 proof of purchase (liner or label) from York, Smoothy or Crunchy Peanut Butter to: Star Wars Poster Offer, Box 41, Station 'G', Toronto, Ontario M4M 3E8. Offer expires January 1, 1981.

2. C-3PO et R2-D2 attendent avec anxiété des nouvelles de Luke Skywalker, perdu dans les vastes plaines gelées de Hoth.

OFFRE D'AFFICHE 'STAR WARS'™
Affiche spéciale en couleurs 'Star Wars' représentant **Darth Vader** en action. Dimension: 16X20 pouces. Pour commander l'affiche, veuillez envoyer un chèque ou mandat-poste de $2.00 payable à: Offre d'affiche 'Star Wars' accompagné d'une preuve d'achat (parchemin ou étiquette) d'un bocal de beurre d'arachides York, Smoothy ou Crunchy à: Offre d'affiche 'Star Wars', Case postale 41, Succursale 'G', Toronto, Ontario, M4M 3E8. L'offre prend fin le 1er janvier 1981.

TM: ©LFL 1980/Canada Packers Inc., authorized user.
TM: ©LFL 1980/Usager autorisé: Canada Packers Inc.

Facsimile © 1998 Lucasfilm Ltd.

CHAPTER II PRODUCTIONS LTD.

Call Sheet No: 12
(Studio)

PRODUCTION: "THE EMPIRE STRIKES BACK"   DATE: Wednesday, 28th March, 1979.

DIRECTOR: IRVIN KERSHNER   UNIT CALL: 08.30 hrs.

SETS: STAGE 1
1. INT. COMMAND CENTRE/ICE CORRIDOR
2. INT. MAIN ICE TUNNEL

ARTISTE:	CHARACTER:	D/R:	M/UP:	READY:

1) INT. COMMAND CENTRE/ICE CORRIDOR: Scs. 178pt., 182, T205, 15 to comp.

ARTISTE:	CHARACTER:	D/R:	M/UP:	READY:
CARRIE FISHER	LEIA	76/78	7.00	8.30
HARRISON FORD	HAN	86/88	8.00	8.30
ANTHONY DANIELS	THREEPIO	129	8.15	8.30
DAVE PROWSE	DARTH VADER	133	9.00 for rehearsal	
KENNY BAKER	ARTOO	131	S/BY at home T.B.A.	
JERRY HARTE	HEAD CONTROLLER		TO BE ADVISED	

STAND-INS:
LIZ COKE	for Ms. Fisher)			
JACK DEARLOVE	for Mr. Ford)		8.00	8.30
ALAN HARRIS	for Mr. Daniels)			
MURRAY BUSH	for Mr. Prowse)			

CROWD:
3 MEN } REBELS			8.00	8.30
2 WOMEN }			7.30	8.30
15 SNOW TROOPERS			8.30	9.00
CHRIS PARSONS	WHITE THREEPIO		8.30	9.00

STUNT ARTISTES:
PETER DIAMOND	Stunt Co-ordinator		S/BY from 8.30	

PROPS: Com-link for Han. Weapons for rebels and snow troops.

ART DEPT: Falling ice – large section to fall Sc. T205.

SP.FX: Steam/Spark fx. Cave in/explosion fx.

MEDICAL: Nurse to S/BY on set from 8.30 a.m.

2) INT. MAIN ICE TUNNEL: Sc. 25

ARTISTE:	CHARACTER:	D/R:	M/UP:	READY:
HARRISON FORD	HAN		From above	
RAY HASSETT	DECK OFFICER		TO BE ADVISED	
NORWICH DUFF	2ND OFFICER		TO BE ADVISED	

STAND-IN:
JACK DEARLOVE	for Mr. Ford		From above	

CROWD:
10 REBEL SOLDIER			8.30	9.00
5 REBEL SOLDIERS			From above	

PROPS: All Tauntaun equipment, weapons for Rebel Soldiers, droid thermometer. Broken Hardware.

SP.FX: Medical droid.

ART DEPT: 1. Pool of water   2. Dead Tauntaun fx.

MAKE-UP: 1. Special Tauntaun head reqd.   2. Tauntaun feet reqd.

TESTS/REHEARSALS

1. Mark Hamill – fencing from 10 a.m.
2. Billy Dee Williams – Wardrobe fitting at Berman's 10 a.m.
3. Blue Screen Test – Stage 8
4. Audition: Cloud city Men/Women – 10.30 a.m. (EMI – Stage 1 & 2)

TRANSPORT:
1. P. Lewsey to P/UP Ms. Fisher @ 6.20 to arrive by 7.00.
2. P. Ferretti to P/UP Mr. Ford @ 7.30 to arrive by 8 a.m.
3. D. Cressy to P/UP Mr. Daniels @ 7.45 to arrive by 8.15 a.m.
4. R. Najda to P/UP Mr. Hamill @ 9.15 to EMI Studios.
5. L. Furseddon to P/UP Billy Dee Williams @ 9.30 & to Bermans

For the first televised airing of the Japanese-dubbed version of Star Wars on October 5, 1983, the Nihon Television network provided this promotional paper-and-plastic fan to subscribers of the Yomiuri Shimbun newspaper—although October in Japan doesn't tend to be overly hot.

CHAPTER III COMPANY—A Subsidiary of Lucasfilm Ltd.
P.O. BOX 2009, SAN RAFAEL, CALIFORNIA 94912 TELEPHONE (000)000/0000 TELEX: 000-000 LFL SRFL

Return of the Jedi *had a couple of other titles before it was anointed with the final version. Lucasfilm feared, rightly so, that fans would try to mob the set if they knew that some shooting was taking place outdoors on public land in Arizona and California. So it came up with a phony film through which it made all its arrangements, Blue Harvest, which even had an ad line on crew T-shirts: "Horror Beyond Imagination." Here is stationery for it and* Revenge of the Jedi, *which was made by Chapter III Company.*

P.O. Box 2009, San Rafael, California 94912   Telephone (000) 000-0000

Telex: 000000 LFLPROD SRFL

A never-used Revenge of the Jedi *action-figure card backing for the popular bounty hunter, Boba Fett. Kenner had to destroy thousands of such cards when George Lucas changed the film's title late in 1982, but some survived.*

The Star Wars™
saga continues...

STAR WARS
REVENGE OF THE
JEDI™

To be released May 25, 1983

STAR WARS
REVENGE OF THE
JEDI™

Be on the lookout for new toys from the Star Wars: Revenge of the Jedi™ Collection:

• 17 New Action Figures • New Playsets • New Vehicles • New Toys from the Star Wars™ Micro Collection™ **COMING SOON...**

ROJ-40

If you liked the cantina scene in Star Wars, *then you loved the denizens of Jabba the Hutt's palace in* Return of the Jedi. *Instead of having to rush and take pre-existing masks off the shelf, Lucasfilm was able to spend more than a year developing new creatures, such as this motley crew surrounding a befuddled C-3PO aboard Jabba's barge, all in a publicity still from Twentieth Century-Fox Film.*

PROJECTIONIST PLEASE NOTE

THIS FEATURE PRINT

"STAR WARS"

INCLUDES A SPECIAL
ADVANCE TRAILER FOR

REVENGE OF THE JEDI

NAME OF ADVANCE TRAILER FILM

90 SECONDS
RUNNING TIME OF
TRAILER

'121 MIN.
RUNNING TIME OF
FEATURE

Please Do Not Edit Or Remove From Print

20th CENTURY FOX TM

The 1982 rerelease of Star Wars carried with it a special goodie, a 90-second advance trailer for Revenge of the Jedi, as seen in this image. Soon after the title—and all the trailers—were changed.

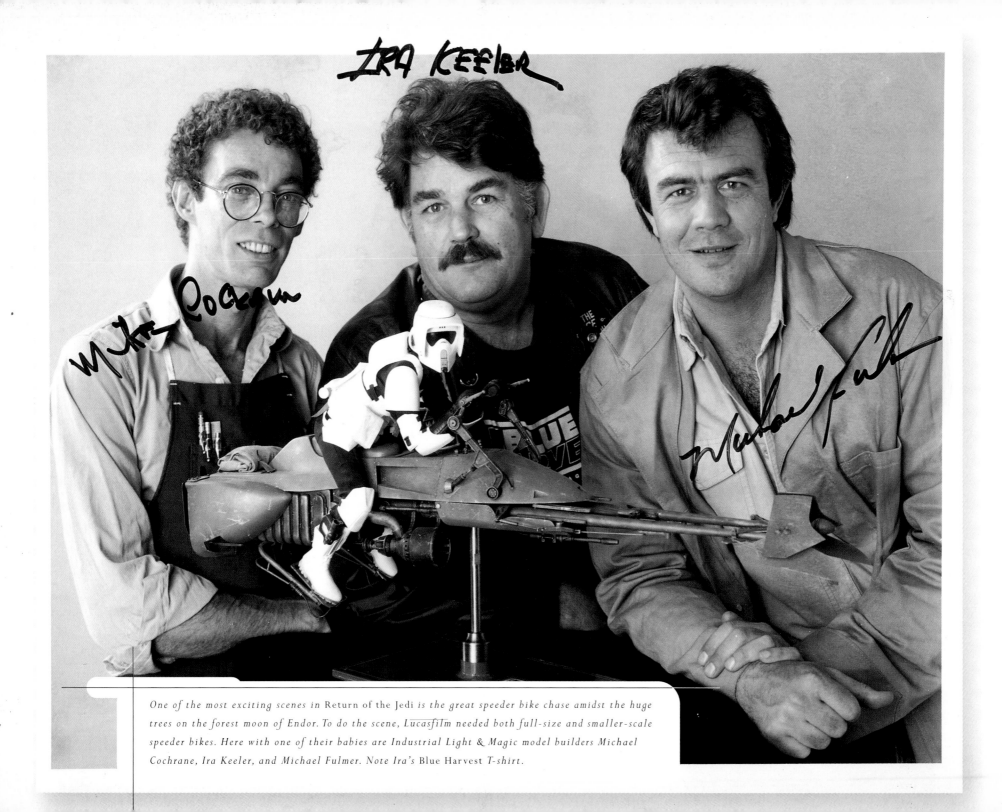

One of the most exciting scenes in Return of the Jedi *is the great speeder bike chase amidst the huge trees on the forest moon of Endor. To do the scene, Lucasfilm needed both full-size and smaller-scale speeder bikes. Here with one of their babies are Industrial Light & Magic model builders Michael Cochrane, Ira Keeler, and Michael Fulmer. Note Ira's* Blue Harvest *T-shirt.*

What could be more exciting, after working on Return of the Jedi
for nearly three years, than to open an envelope and get your
engraved invitation to see the fruits of your labors on the big
screen with other members of the crew? My friends tell me that the
10 a.m. screening at the Coronet Theatre and the buffet lunch at
Maxwell's Plum that followed were real celebrations.

THE SAGA CONTINUES.

STAR WARS
RETURN OF THE JEDI

スター・ウォーズ
ジェダイの復讐

An advance chirashi, or Japanese handbill, from March 1983 for the premiere of Return of the Jedi (at least in English, although the Japanese characters still spell out Revenge of the Jedi). The art, from the U.S. advance poster, is by famed illustrator Drew Struzan.

JEDI KNIGHT T.M.

CERTIFICATE

HONORARY JEDI KNIGHT CERTIFICATE

Let it be known to all in the Galaxy that

is hereby enrolled in The Order of Honorary Jedi Knights

"May The Force be with you" T.M.

I, Yoda, the Jedi Master, T.M.
affix my signature

Yoda

STAR WARS

RETURN OF THE JEDI ™

"A Jedi's strength flows from the Force"

And you thought it was difficult to become a Jedi Knight! Not at all, at least to become an honorary Jedi. All you had to do was purchase a pair of Star Wars Underoos — ranging from Luke to Leia to Yoda underwear — and cut out this certificate from inside the front of the package. What if Luke had known it was that easy?

Underwear that's Fun to Wear!

Polyester and cotton blend for comfort and fit

Colorfast

Needs no ironing

Shrinkage controlled

Heat resistant waistband

Lycra* spandex leg openings

WASHING INSTRUCTIONS

- Machine wash—<u>warm</u> setting.
- Tumble dry—<u>low</u> setting.
- For best results wash inside out.
- Do <u>not</u> bleach.
- Do <u>not</u> iron or dry-clean emblem.

SIZE	AGE	WEIGHT	HEIGHT
small (2-4)	up to 3 yrs.	up to 46 lbs.	up to 40"
medium (6-8)	4-6 yrs.	47-61 lbs.	41"-50"
large (10-12)	7-9 yrs.	62-89 lbs.	51"-59"

Guarantee

This garment is boys' underwear and is intended for use as underwear, not sleepwear. As an underwear product, it meets the Federal Flammability Standards applicable to all children's clothing other than sleepwear.

A PRODUCT OF AMERICA'S LARGEST MANUFACTURER OF QUALITY UNDERWEAR

UNION UNDERWEAR COMPANY, INC.
P.O. BOX 780
BOWLING GREEN, KY 42101

wear that's Fun to Wear!

PAULS

POPSICLES

STAR WARS

10 PACK

STAR WARS

780ml.

ICE CONFECTION

INGREDIENTS:
CANE SUGAR, FOOD ACID,
VEGETABLE GUMS,
FLAVOURS, COLOURS,
WATER ADDED.

ARTIFICIALLY COLOURED
AND FLAVOURED.

STORE AT OR
BELOW -18°C

USE BY

ASSORTED FLAVOURS

9 310080 020883

Star Wars trilogy images have graced food packaging around the globe, but perhaps never more attractively than on this 1983 box of ten assorted Popsicles from Pauls in Australia. An artist for Australian United Foods modified Tom Jung's original Star Wars poster for the front of the box and took an image from Jung's art for the rare half sheet poster to come up with this striking design.

If you ate all those Star Wars candies and ice cream treats, you'd better be sure to brush your teeth. And what better way to do it than with Star Wars toothbrushes, these from a 1983 salesman's sample kit and brochure from the Oral-B unit of CooperCare. "Order today," the brochure implored, "and may the profits be with you!"

Ann Sachs and Perry King (center) join original film cast members Anthony Daniels (right) and Billy Dee Williams (left) while taping National Public Radio's THE EMPIRE STRIKES BACK. The new 10-part series is produced by NPR in association with KUSC/Los Angeles and with the cooperation of Lucasfilm Ltd. NPR member station   will present the intergalactic adventure on   at   .m.,
beginning   (Photo credit: Mary Ellen Mark/Archive Photo)

Kenner's Power of the Force action-figure line was supposed to be at least sixty-two figures strong, but as sales started declining two years after the release of Return of the Jedi, only a little more than half of that number made it onto cards with collectible aluminum coins.

Some cards were printed but never released, such as this one for Admiral Ackbar. There were unreleased coins for unreleased figures in the separate Droids and Ewoks cartoon lines (from top) such as Admiral Screed and Morag; a prototype, smaller Luke Jedi coin; an unproduced sixty-third coin that was to come in goldtone with a collectors' coin album; and error coins, such as this one for Jabba's Sail Barge, corrected later to Sail Skiff.

You can see *Star Wars* on the screen, but you can ride it only at the four Disney parks around the world. Each has a *Star Tours* simulator attraction. The first opened at California's Disneyland in 1987, and the "flight material" for the press included a plastic "credit card." *Star Tours* shared its opening at Florida's Disney World with the opening of the Swan Hotel (one of several different color press badges).

STAR TOURS
BOARDING PASS

101

TURE DISNEYLAND TOMORROWLAND SPACEPORT

IATION: MOON OF ENDOR

DATES: JANUARY 8 & 9, 1987

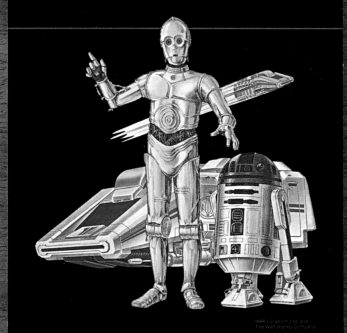

STAR TOURS
TRAVEL AGENCY
Disneyland

STAR TOURS
Disneyland
JANUARY 1987

© 1986 Lucasfilm Ltd. and The Walt Disney Company

STAR TOURS
WALT DISNEY WORLD SWAN

Walt Disney World®

FLIGHT MATERIAL

JOIN THIS ONCE IN A LIFETIME EVENT

creation Conventions
presents

STARLOG® SALUTES STAR WARS®

A 10th Anniversary Tribute to George Lucas and the Galaxy Far, Far Away Which He Created!

MAY 23, 24, 25, 1987 Memorial Day Weekend

STOUFFER CONCOURSE HOTEL • 5400 W. CENTURY BLVD.
LOS ANGELES, CALIFORNIA

**A Weekend of Galactic Entertainment
That You Won't Want To Miss!!!**

B A N T H A   T R A C K S

NUMBER 35
WINTER 1987

JOURNAL OF THE OFFICIAL **STAR WARS/LUCASFILM** FAN CLUB

10TH ANNIVERSARY ISSUE

INSIDE

GALA STAR TOURS RIBBON CUTTING AT DISNEYLAND

Not With Scissors — With A Light Saber

Sparks shot and smoke poured into the air as STAR WARS characters danced across a huge stage set up at the entrance to Disneyland's Tomorrowland for the grand opening ceremonies of STAR TOURS — George Lucas' thrilling new attraction that puts you in the STAR WARS Universe.

DARTH VADER watched as the EWOKS defeated the Empire's Storm Troopers, all live and on stage — watched and recorded by hundreds of video crews from all over

continued inside . . . .

With the wave of a light saber, George Lucas and Michael Eisner officially open STAR TOURS. Seconds later, sparks flew and a blizzard of mylar confetti filled the sky.

JOE CHURCH

© 1987 THE WALT DISNEY COMPANY

The Tenth Anniversary issue of the Official Star Wars/Lucasfilm Fan Club newsletter, Bantha Tracks, was also its last. After thirty-five issues, it was time to call it a day (actually about nine years) with an issue that celebrated the opening of Star Tours and included a Tenth Anniversary fold-out poster. Happily, a new licensed fan club magazine quickly followed.

May — STAR WARS first anniversary poster is issued.

July — The Official STAR WARS Fan Club issues its first newsletter.

July 21 — STAR WARS is re-released (for the first time).

November 17 — THE STAR WARS HOLIDAY SPECIAL airs on CBS-TV featuring CHEWBACCA & THE WOOKIES.

1979

March 5 — THE EMPIRE STRIKES BACK commences photography in Finse, Norway; and later in England; through September 24.

March — The STAR WARS comic strip by Russ Manning begins syndication through the L.A. Times in 214 newspapers.

Special Effects for EMPIRE are created at ILM all through 1979 into the spring of 1980.

August 15 — STAR WARS re-released for the second time.

November 11 — The Art of STAR WARS book is published starting a unique publishing trend. The "Art of . . ." books from all three films remain in print even today in 1987, years beyond the theatrical life of the films which is highly unusual.

May 19 — DARTH VADER makes the cover of TIME Magazine.

May 21 — THE EMPIRE STRIKES BACK is released nationwide in the U.S.

EMPIRE STRIKES BACK

May — The soundtrack album of STAR WARS has already sold 3 million copies by this date and the paperback novelization over 5 million.

The novelization of EMPIRE has already sold 2 million copies by the end of the first week of the film's release. It was #4 on the *New York Times* paperback bestseller list on May 18 before the film's release.

The soundtrack of EMPIRE has sold 800,000 copies at same point.

Adweek claims on May 12 that Kenner had retail sales of $100,000,000 on STAR WARS toys in each of the years 1978 and 1979.

May — EMPIRE breaks 125 out of 127 house records for opening day, a new industry high for the highest single day per theater gross representing completely sold out business.

June 9 — YODA makes the cover of PEOPLE Magazine.

1981

January — YODA is parodied on the cover of MAD Magazine.

YODA is among others on the cover of LIFE Magazine's special Year In Pictures issue for 1980.

April 10 — STAR WARS is re-released for the third time.

April — EMPIRE wins two Academy Awards (for the year 1980) for: Best Sound and Special Achievement for Visual Effects.

July 31 — EMPIRE is re-released for the first time.

September 5 — The STAR WARS Radiodrama begins on National Public radio, 13 episodes in all.

1983

February 17-18 — The EMPIRE STRIKES BACK Radiodrama, a 10-part series commences on National Public Radio.

February — STAR WARS shown on cable TV.

May 23 — George Lucas makes the cover of TIME Magazine.

STAR WARS RETURN OF THE JEDI

July 4 — Time capsule is placed in the foundation at Skywalker Ranch. Included in the capsule is a microfilmed list of the STAR WARS Fan Club's members.

August 13 — STAR WARS is re-released for the fourth time.

November 19 — EMPIRE is re-released for the second time.

June — LIFE Magazine features "The Father of the JEDI," a cover story about George Lucas and his creations.

April — RETURN OF THE JEDI wins an Academy Award (for 1983) for: Special Visual Effects.

May 16 — George Lucas and Steven Spielberg place their footprints in the cement at Mann's Chinese Theater in Hollywood.

1985 represents the 7th year of the STAR WARS Kenner line, the[best] selling line of boys toys in history. (For this purpose[...] WARS is considered a[...]

1986

February 1 — EMPIRE [...] in cable TV.

February 25 — JEDI comes [on] video cassette.

September 13 — THE [...] EWOKS second seas[on ...] tion commences on ABC-TV[...]

THE FIRST TEN YEARS

STAR WARS

1977   1987

November — THE EMPIRE STRIKES BACK comes out on video cassette.

November 25 — THE EWOK ADVENTURE airs on ABC-TV as a made-for-TV movie.

1985

March 28 — First triple-bill screening of the trilogy (STAR WARS, EMPIRE and JEDI) in a one-day eight-city event.

March 29 — RETURN OF THE JEDI is re-released.

September 7 — THE EWOK ADVENTURE wins an Emmy Award for Outstanding Visual Effects.

September 7 — THE EWOK & DROIDS ADVENTURE HOUR, the first season of animation, commences on ABC on Saturday mornings.

November 24 — EWOKS: THE BATTLE FOR ENDOR airs on ABC-TV.

June 11 — The *New York Times* Best Seller List includes 5 JEDI books at the same time. The JEDI Storybook is #1 on the hardcover list; the JEDI Novelization is #1 on [...]

1987

January 9 — STAR TOURS [...] from Disneyland in Anaheim[...] nia with George Lucas and Michael Eisner cutt[ing ...] the Grand Ope[ning ...]

STAR TOURS
Tokyo Disneyland

STAR TOURS GALAXY PARTY
TUESDAY, JULY 11, 1989

"スター・ツアーズ プレスプレビュー"のご案内

未体験のスペース・アドベンチャー"スター・ツアーズ"が、きたる7月12日(水)、「東京ディズニーランド」にオープンいたします。これに先立ちまして、7月11日(火)、報道関係者のみなさまを対象として、下記の通りプレスプレビューを開催いたしますので、なにとぞ、ご取材たまわりますようお願い申し上げます。

また、当日は、7:00P.M.より、各界著名の方々をお招きしての"スター・ツアーズ ギャラクシーパーティー"を予定いたしております。スペシャル・エンターテイメントも準備いたしておりますので、あわせてご取材いただければ幸いでございます。

プレスプレビュー&ギャラクシーパーティー タイムスケジュール

プレスプレビュー(於:スター・ツアーズ)
2:00P.M.〜 5:00P.M.　記者発表(於:ショーベース2000)
5:00P.M.〜 5:45P.M.　トゥモローランド・テラス、プラザ・レストラン
6:00P.M.〜 7:00P.M.　にお食事の用意をいたしております。

7:00P.M.〜10:00P.M.　ギャラクシーパーティー(於:トゥモローランド)

Reporters in Tokyo, and my friend Eimei, got this elegant pop-up invitation to a Star Tours "Galaxy Party" to celebrate the opening of the ride at Tokyo Disneyland in the summer of 1989.

The Star Wars Trilogy Special Edition *brought millions of old fans and an equal number of new ones back to movie theaters around the world to experience the thrills and excitement of the galactic saga. And who could see them only once? The All Access badge let Lucasfilm and Twentieth Century-Fox employees get past the barriers at the world premiere in the Westwood section of Los Angeles. But the place to see the films was in Hollywood at Mann's Chinese Theater with two thousand other screaming fans at special screenings the nights before each one opened.*

STAR WARS
SPECIAL EDITION

PERSON AND IS

LUCASFILM LTD. PRESENTS YOUR TICKET TO THE SCREENING OF

STAR WARS™
SPECIAL EDITION

Saturday Morning ▲ January 25 ▲ 9:30AM
at
Pacific's Rowland Theatre
44 Rowland Way ▲ Novato

THIS TICKET ADMITS ONE (1) PERSON AND IS NON-TRANSFERABLE

▲ February 15 ▲ 9:30AM
at
...ronet Theatre
...levard ▲ San Francisco

STRIKES EDITION

February 15 ▲ 9:...
at
...gency Cinema
...Road ▲ San Rafa...
IS NON-TRANSFE...

LUCASFILM LTD. PRESENTS YOUR TICKET TO THE SCREENING OF

THE EMPIRE STRIKES BACK™
SPECIAL EDITION

Saturday Morning ▲ February 15 ▲ 9:30AM
at
Pacific's Cinema...

LUCASFILM LTD. PRESENTS YOUR TICKET TO THE SCREENING OF

THE EMPIRE STRIKES BACK™

...RABLE

...SENTS YOUR TICK...

LUCASFILM LTD. PRESENTS YOUR TICKET TO THE SCREENING OF

THE RETURN OF THE JEDI™
SPECIAL EDITION

LUCASFILM LTD. PRESENTS YOUR TICKET TO THE SCREENING OF

THE RETURN OF THE JEDI™
SPECIAL EDITION

Saturday Morning ▲ March 1 ▲ 9:30AM
at
...cifi... Reg...y Cin...a
...San Rafael...

AM
...CO
...ABLE

STAR
SPECIAL EDITION

SPECIAL EDITION

Saturday M...

THE RETURN OF TH...

THIS TICKET ADMITS

While in Australia attending Force II, the Star Walking fan club convention in June 1997, I went on a chip-buying frenzy. The prettiest bag—with the tastiest snack—was for BBQ Stars. And the free Techno Tazo inside each bag wasn't bad either, only you needed fifty different Tazos for a complete set. Which accounts for the chip-buying frenzy.

NORWEGIAN UNIT

STAR WARS

THE FIRST
1977 STAR WARS 1987
©LFL
TEN YEARS

STAR WARS
THE
EMPIRE
STRIKES BACK

Embroidered cloth patches make wonderful collectibles because they are easy to store and often have a story attached. The set on the left was worn by the first crew members to venture to the frozen land of Finse, Norway, before Star Wars II even had a name. The "Vader in Flames" patch came next (although perhaps it should have been saved for the third movie where, at the end, Vader's helmet actually goes up in flames). The First Ten Years patch was sold at the fabled anniversary convention in Los Angeles.

The unusual design of the letters on the blue
Star Wars patch shows it to be the very first
crew patch made for the film.

The starry Star Wars patch was one of
the first sold commercially.

The Revenge patches were quickly replaced by patches with the film's new title. The Kenner patches were for promotions and are very rare.

MAY THE FORCE BE WITH YOU

STAR WARS

FACTORS ETC. INC., D. IMAGE FACTORY INC., CA. • © 1977 TWENTIETH CENTURY FOX FILM CORP.

STAR WARS

A short time ahead in a Kingdom very, very near...

STAR TOURS

DARTH VADAR LIVES

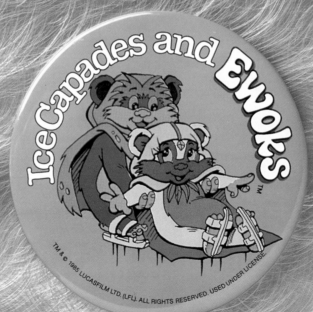

IceCapades and Ewoks

TM & © 1985 LUCASFILM LTD. (LFL). ALL RIGHTS RESERVED. USED UNDER LICENSE.

THE STAR WARS TRILOGY

March 28, 1985

There are hundreds of pinback badges relating to the Star Wars

STAR WARS TRILOGY
IN A THX THEATRE
FOR THE VERY FIRST TIME.

STAR WARS
MAY THE FORCE BE WITH YOU
Kenner

YODA GOES PUBLIC.
NATIONAL PUBLIC RADIO

STAR WARS TRILOGY
ON VIDEO AUGUST 29

An early Kenner promotional button joins Yoda, promoting The Empire Strikes Back dramatization on National Public Radio. The Vader button is for the 1995 sale of the trilogy on remastered video, while the rectangular button was worn by ushers and refreshment stand workers at THX certified theaters that showed the Special Edition.

本年度アカデミー賞7部門受賞
■音楽賞 ■美術賞 ■衣裳デザイン賞 ■編集賞
■録音賞 ■視覚効果賞 ■特殊音響効果賞

MAY THE FORCE BE WITH YOU

STAR WARS
スター・ウォーズ

20世紀フォックス提供　ルーカス・フイルムLTD作品
スター・ウォーズ
主演マーク・ハミル／ハリソン・フォード／キャリー・フィッシャー
ピーター・カッシング
アレック・ギネス
脚本・監督　製作　音楽
ジョージ・ルーカス　ゲイリー・カーツ　ジョン・ウィリアムス
パナビジョンⓇ　テクニカラーⓇ
〈オリジナル・サントラ盤〉20世紀レコード▯▯ DOLBY SYSTEM
原作ジョージ・ルーカス（角川書店刊）
© 1977 20TH CENTURY-FOX

特別優待割引券

（同時上映　ルパン三世）
★本券ご持参の方に限り
〈劇場窓口〉一般500円／学生400円のところ
一般400円
学生300円 ｝に割引いたします
★この券1枚にて3名様有効
4月28日(土)ぉ5月14日(月)まで上映

伊勢丹
新館となり　テアトル新宿 (352)
1846

It's Back!
──いま、帰って来る──

日本語版
STAR WARS
スター・ウォーズ

20世紀フォックス提供
松竹株式会社・配給
ルーカス・フイルムLTD作品
マーク・ハミル
ハリソン・フォード
キャリー・フィッシャー
監督・脚本・原作
ジョージ・ルーカス
※第50回アカデミー賞
7部門受賞作品

特別ご鑑賞券　¥1200

STAR WARS シリーズ第3弾
──完結篇！──

スター・ウォーズ
ジェダイの復讐

STAR WARS
RETURN OF THE JEDI
FOX映画

©Lucasfilm Ltd. Twentieth Century Fox

特別割引券

8月20日(土)より9月22日(木)まで
○本券ご持参の方に限り、窓口表示料金より
大人・学生200円、小人100円割引致します。
（1枚で3名様有効）

松原団地駅東口前
東武　松原シネマ2
☎ 0489(35)†301

THE BATTLE FOR ENDOR
presents
GEORGE LUCAS

ジョージ・ルーカス作品

エンドア　魔空の妖怪

Unlike the boring ticket stubs at American theaters, the Japanese advance discount tickets and coupons get poster and other art for the opening of new films. In fact, it's a major hobby in Japan to collect and trade these beautiful miniatures, with shows and even books published about them. Here are two my friend Eimei saved for me from Star Wars (the second for the Japanese-dubbed version in 1982), and one each from Return of the Jedi and the Ewok movie, The Battle for Endor.

Producer Gary Kurtz was big on having imprinted items promoting the films, including the Star Wars adhesive name badge and The Empire Strikes Back drink coasters. They'd be perfect for Aunt Beru's blue milk!

Sweet on Star Wars? It's hard not to be, especially in Europe, which has a long tradition of parents buying their children sweet treats every day, such as these British Burton's Biscuits bags that contained mini chocolate chip cookies. The ice cream sticks from Frigo in Spain are part of a set of 18—but the image of Obi-Wan Kenobi was nearly impossible to find since it could be redeemed for a Kenner toy. The four French cards are from a game, Jedi Challenge, and were inside the cookie wrapper from Biscuiterie Nantaise. All are from 1997.

These Australian ice cream treat wrappers have a graphic look that reminds me of the early stone lithographed movie posters of the 1920s. But I'm not sure I want a frozen confection filled with "Jedi Jelly."

The world lives on snack foods, including a Lyons Maid chocolate iced lolly from England, a Nestlé's Crunch bar from the U.S., an ice cream bar wrapper from Malaysia, and my personal favorite, a label from Finland for a bottle of Yoda Soda.

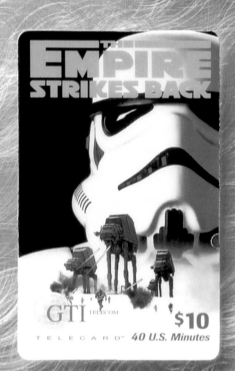

IMPERIAL PROBE DROID

LA GUERRE
L'EMPIRE
CONTRE-ATTAQUE
DES ETOILES ™

offert par PAPOU et PALMITO

TM © Lucasfilm LTD. (LFL) 1980
extension 21 — printed in Italy

STAR
WARS
™

The unusual embossed plastic trading card above
is from a French series. At top right is one of a set
of thirty cards from Japan's Yamakatsu under license
from Topps. The bottom card is one of a series that
came inside Myojo noodle cups in Japan. I have
been trying to add to the few in my collection for
more than a decade, but they are very scarce and
I personally know of no one with a complete set.

There were one hundred *Return of the Jedi* miniature trading cards from the Netherlands; the wrapper is below. The 1985 Spanish *Droids* set has images taken directly from the animated television series.

STAR WARS
RETURN OF THE JEDI

14.

3.

STAR WARS
RETURN OF THE JEDI

STAR WARS
RETURN OF THE JEDI

22.

STAR WARS
RETURN OF THE JEDI

For years, Lucasfilm marked Christmas by sending Star Wars holiday-themed Christmas cards, not available to the general public. Nearly all of these were painted by the original concept artist, Ralph McQuarrie. One, with C-3PO and Santa before a cozy fire, was used as the cover art for the Star Wars Christmas Album.

Happy Holidays